SO
YOU
WANT
TO BE
AN
ELECTRICIAN?

Your complete guide to the electrical industry

GARY ALDER

SO YOU WANT TO BE AN ELECTRICIAN?

ISBN 978-1-915962-32-4
First published by Compass-Publishing UK 2024

Printed in the United Kingdom

A catalogue version of the book can be found at the British Library

Interior layout by The Book Refinery Ltd
www.TheBookRefinery.com

Cover designed by © Peter Lampridis

Author photo © Beth Haslam

For Mel, Without your years of love and support,
none of this would be possible!

CONTENTS

INTRODUCTION

For thousands of people every year, choosing to become an electrician can be the most important decision they make. Not everyone who starts this journey will finish it. It's a commitment we all make to spend our careers, or even our lives, striving for: to be the *complete* electrical engineer.

The electrical industry is a vast, confusing place. Through its myriad of governance structures and memberships, the fundamentals of wielding "bottled lightning" remain the same.

Since the first edition of the *Rules and Regulations* was published in 1882, the electrical industry has been on an exponential journey of development. Here we are, over 140 years later, now implementing technologies that were once thought of as futuristic and that Nikola Tesla could only dream of.

The routes of employment within the electrical industry are just as numerous as the technologies we use: you may be employed, be self-employed, run a limited company or be an agency worker. Almost all types of employment are available to you when you enter the industry. Each one has its own positives and negatives (pardon the pun).

Whether we're self-employed or run a limited company, we must all navigate the same economics, dealing with issues such as contracts, employment, taxes and payroll to name but a few. Becoming familiar with these is equally as important as the engineering work you'll undertake every day.

Job titles can be just as creative as in the rest of the world when it comes to a person's curriculum vitae (CV). Qualifications are wide ranging and issued by various bodies. The combination of creative job titles and an industry littered with an assortment of equivalent qualifications makes it a minefield to determine someone's competence.

The skills of managing contracts, people and budgets are necessities for anyone wishing to succeed in the construction industry, regardless of their employment status. A fundamental, underpinning knowledge of these soft skills is as critical to success as any engineering knowledge attained during your career.

Legislation has always been key in keeping both workers and customers safe. The Electricity at Work Act 1989 and the Health and Safety at Work Act 1974 have maintained a safety baseline for the electrical industry since their creation. Understanding safety for our own and others' well-being is fundamental to the training electricians undertake. Whether it's gaining competence in the production or reading of documentation, such as risk assessments or method statements, staying safe is always *the* priority.

This industry is littered with competent person schemes, trade bodies, certification bodies, memberships, companies, charities and committees. Navigating these to ensure you comply with the appropriate legislation is a must for anyone wishing to operate within or run their own business in this subsection of construction.

The electrical industry is developing continuously, as must the engineers and electricians alike who are at the forefront of it.

Training is at the centre of everything electricians do, whether it's having a fundamental understanding of the regulations or exploring the new technologies creeping into the sector.

Human beings have undertaken apprenticeships for thousands of years. Whether it's known by a different name or not, the passing down of skills from one generation to the next is what's made humanity different to all other species on this planet.

With the industry now looking towards renewable energy, home generation and electric vehicles (EVs), electricians' skills must be as wide ranging domestically as they've been historically at an industrial level. Apprenticeships, training and continuous professional development (CPD) are all key to this. It's clear that the fate of billions of humans on this planet lie in the hands of engineers and electricians. Every single one of us has our part to play.

How to Read This Book

Whilst this book may contain many chapters that will seem confusing for the person who knows very little about the electrical industry, this book is structured to take you through your journey from apprenticeship to what's beyond, so it will be most beneficial to read it in order. At the back, there are handy abbreviations broken down for any aspect that you might not have learned yet.

For those of you who've picked up this book who already have more experience of the electrical industry, you might be able to roam through the chapters of this book more freely.

CHAPTER 1

APPRENTICESHIPS

Employers

There are many ways to enter the electrical industry. The key words and phrases you'll discover on starting this journey will include, in one form or another, the word "apprenticeship". This means not only being educated within a formal classroom setting but also gaining experience on the job. Implementing the knowledge you've gained during your college tuition is the very essence of an apprenticeship.

Apprenticeships have been on a downward trajectory in recent years. The industry has experienced more apprentices leaving college during their first year than there have been historically. There doesn't appear to be a single reason for this, but it's an issue that can be debated long into the night. However, this doesn't mean to say that completing an apprenticeship isn't a perfectly viable option for many.

There are many things to consider when embarking on an apprenticeship. One at the top of the list should be the employer. When selecting an employer, which is potentially your very first employer, the decision must be treated with the same degree of care as the educational selection made by someone who's choosing their A levels en route to university. Both will guide you down a long path with years of education, training and, ultimately, qualifications ahead of you when moving into the world of employment.

When the world's economies are turbulent, gaining employment can sometimes feel like a victory in and of itself. However, aligning your employer to your own principles is key. Whether you're legally an adult or not, this shouldn't and doesn't matter when entering the world of employment.

It's also crucial to consider what you want to achieve during your apprenticeship, though this is a period of reflection that most won't undertake and that many won't do until later in life (but we'll come back to that). Asking the right questions at the interview stage can help you to avoid a potentially painful experience.

Initially, you can look at some of the work that the potential employer tends to undertake. Are they a domestic, commercial or industrial-based contractor? Bearing in mind that electricians must take an appropriate national vocational qualification (NVQ), you should understand that a healthy variety of work is needed.

You can also look at their workforce (if they have one). Who else do they employ? Having long-standing staff shows good staff retention, loyalty and, to some degree, success.

Historically, apprentices have been the ones who'd be the first to crawl into the spider-ridden loft spaces, wading through the itchy loft insulation, and chasing the brickwork with a hammer and bolster, barely visible through the dust. Many employers will still operate in this manner, as there is value to it. The compensating thought is that every electrician instructing an apprentice will, at some point, have had to do it themselves. It's a rite of passage, if you will.

Your contract can also tell you a great deal about the employer; whilst trial periods are common for all workplaces, extending this beyond a typical three-month period could be deemed unreasonable and a potential warning sign that they're using cheaper, short-term labour. If there's a lack of work, then as an employee, you can manipulate this to your benefit too – some work is better than no work! It's key to remember that a trial period is as much about you trialling the employer as it is about them trialling you. Ensuring respect is given is a two-way street that not all employers will feel apprentices deserve.

Some contractors may operate on a zero-hours basis and only pay for hours worked. Others may pay you a salary. The number of days holiday you're offered is always key: how much does the employer value the rest-and-relaxation part of their staff's lives?

Burnout is real, and some employers may have a lack of understanding that you – as an employee – aren't financially invested in a business and so don't want to work every waking hour; this may confuse or even upset some employers. Apprentices are sometimes relied upon to provide this support. There will be some of you who take every opportunity as a learning opportunity, working all hours. To quote the line popularised by Malcolm Gladwell's book *Outliers*: "It takes ten thousand hours of intensive practice to achieve mastery of complex skills and materials."[1] Whilst you may clock these hours up as quickly as you like, it's only when you reflect on your work that you can truly find the benefit of what you've completed in any given working day.

Most employers will now be looking at gaining funding to support them employing apprentices. The one-man bands (people who run a business alone) in particular will see apprentices as a risk and a loss of earnings. There's very much a flipside to this, though. Apprentices need to be viewed as an investment, albeit one that won't pay any dividends for potentially 12–24 months. The time lost in that period can make or break a business, hence the apprehension.

Statistics are often thrown around, but half of all businesses won't make it to their third birthday.[2] Around 60% of small-business start-ups fail due to cash-flow problems,[3] and the construction industry is notoriously one of the worst when it comes to making payments. Whether it's a domestic customer who can't pay until their next pay cheque or a national business with 90-day payment terms, electrical contractors will be funding the materials and labour for projects up and down the country. Whilst some employers will now be taking up-front deposits to avoid late-payment issues from clients, the majority won't operate in this manner, simply to be competitive and to win work. The risk of employing an apprentice will feel like a pressure and responsibility that, until a substantial amount of work is won, they won't commit to.

> It's always good to remember that your employer will have a responsibility to support you.

Attitude

Your personality is who you are, and it factors in to what you'll achieve within the workplace. It can create positive places to work, where lifelong friendships are made and relationships are formed, making it a pleasure to learn and progress into a lifelong career. The workplace can also be the antithesis of this, where you don't want to come to work every day and you hate the job and the mind-numbing work. If you're one of the unfortunate few where this is the case, you're less likely to succeed in the long term.

An enjoyable workplace is as much down to you, the employee, as it is to your employer. However, personalities sometimes just clash. Maturity is a big factor; when most apprentices have just left school, they're doing so as a teenager who's been confined to their social group.

Rule number one is that the working world doesn't care what social group you're in, what your status is or even what trainers you're wearing this week (shocking, I know). It cares that you're performing well at your job, and therefore earning money for everyone related to the project and creating a satisfied, returning customer at its completion.

So many apprentices forget this basic rule. No teenager wants to go back to being subservient and following their employer's rules when they're just breaking free from their parents' and the school's rules. But again, no one cares. If you figure this out quickly, you'll go further and faster.

That can sound harsh when it isn't understood in the proper context. Personal problems and issues should always be always handled and dealt with using the utmost care and respect. However, if you have a metaphorical chip on your shoulder, your apprenticeship isn't going to be the smoothest four-year period of your life. You must be willing to take instruction, make mistakes and learn quickly.

Your attitude is a major factor during your apprenticeship. Being willing to go that extra mile and to listen to the teacher – who, in this instance, is the electrician guiding you through your daily tasks – does pay dividends in the long term.

Another thing to consider is your attitude to making mistakes. A good analogy here would be when smartphones and tablets first came on the market in the 2000s: whilst technophobic parents were scared to use them in case they made an irretrievable mistake, the following generations never held this apprehension after growing up with technology, now operating a tablet from as young as two years old without fear. The parallel with apprenticeships is that, whilst you're learning a new skill, being afraid to make a mistake – perhaps due to not wanting to appear to get something wrong in front of your peers and colleagues – can sometimes cripple you into doing nothing. Rest assured, it's those of us who do push ourselves, make mistakes and move on that are the ones who learn the quickest.

Utilising time outside of work well can provide you (or anyone) with an advantage over others – particularly if you really enjoy what you do. This can be engaging in technical conversations on social media, undertaking webinars, watching simple tutorials from experienced installers online, or even contacting manufacturers to gain a better understanding of their products and get maximum exposure to their benefits.

One simple tip is to always carry a small notebook with you. Nowadays, simply using an app on a mobile phone is incredibly useful; however, I personally feel that you can't beat putting pen to paper. Note-taking is a free way to reflect on the work you're undertaking, and next to no apprentices do this. Keep manufacturers' instructions and file them in the notebook or take a picture – anything like this can help. Then, at the end of each day, review and reflect on what's detailed in the notebook. This doesn't just apply to apprentices but to anyone in a constantly evolving industry where new skills are under development, such as the electrical industry. This is also useful when completing your NVQ. Rather than searching your memory, simply search your notebook.

There are so many clichés present on television and social media that encourage us to seek inspiration to the be the best we can be. If you want to be the best you can be, doing all the little things – taking notes, taking photos, keeping manufacturers' instructions, asking questions and going the extra mile – will help any and every apprentice improve, including electricians. Some may profess to know it all, but trust me, no one does! Following some of these tips this will make you more valuable to any business.

All the Gear, No Idea

It isn't cheap to put together a collection of tools for any trade (commonly known as a "tool bag" on construction sites). There will be many retailers and wholesalers out there who package up trade-specific tools. This is probably one of the more efficient ways to kick start a tool bag. Over time, you can then look to upgrade and replace the tools with newer models.

Typically, funds are low for apprentices when it comes to putting together their first tool bag. Many might want to purchase the latest on-trend screwdriver or hammer, but this may not be possible, and it's more important to have the right tools than the latest ones.

Some key tools you'll need as an apprentice are the following (and don't worry if you haven't a clue what I'm talking about when I get a bit technical in some of these descriptions and elsewhere, as you'll learn all this during your apprenticeship – or you could look it up online):

- **Tool bag** – This is an obvious first choice (from which the whole kit gets its name), but you'll need something to put the tools in. With lots of expensive options available to you, a backpack is the latest go-to product.

- **Screwdrivers** – As an electrician, you'll need all types and sizes of screwdriver, ranging from the large positives and flatheads to the small terminal screwdrivers. They need to be insulated as a minimum for electrical work. A good set can be a worthwhile long-term investment.

- **Side cutters** – If you're dealing with twin and earth cabling, these are probably one of the most useful tools to have. With specific 1.5mm and 2.5mm slots available for cabling terminations, they can assist with cutting and stripping wire. The "half-moons" are also an option for larger cables.

- **Grips** – If you're ever asked to terminate a steel-wired armour cable with a gland, you won't be doing it without two of these.

- **Hacksaw / junior hacksaw** – If you're working with metal containment (aka "metal munching") – such as with tray, ladder and trunking – then a hacksaw is a must. A junior hacksaw is very much a necessity for glanding and assisting with the removal of armouring.

- **Hammer** – If you want to chase walls, clip cables, install fixings, etc., you're going to need a hammer. Some modern hammers even have magnetic nail holders, if you've got cash to splash.

- **Pliers / long-nose pliers** – You'll frequently come across tight terminations and awkward spaces for cabling, and these can assist you in a variety of ways.

- **Knife/knives** – It's common for an electrician's tool bag to contain knives. They're a nuisance and many accidents happen every year as a result. However, they're needed for the glanding element of cabling, and safety equivalents are available.

- **Voltage indicator and proving unit** – A GS38-compliant voltage indicator and proving unit are key items within a safe isolation kit. This might include padlocks, lock outs, warning signs and more to ensure safety when working with live electricity.

- **Tape measure** – This is self-explanatory. You'll need to measure things for many aspects of the job.

- **Set square** – This is a useful tool when measuring and marking out steel containment, whether you're self-manufacturing 90° or 45° bends or simply cutting straight lines.

- **Half-round file** – Again, if you're metal munching your way through containment, rough and sharp edges are frowned upon, so you need a way to remove them.

- **Spirit level** – If you want your sockets, consumer units, containment or anything else to be level, you'll need one of these.

- **Lug/ferrel crimpers** – As an electrician, you'll spend many an hour terminating cabling. Lugs and ferrels facilitate these terminations, so it's vital to have a tool to fix them to the cable. A common task where this would be used is installing main bonding conductors to pipework.

- **Allen keys** – Many fixtures and fittings now incorporate screws with an Allen key head. You could consider getting both metric and imperial, but the latter isn't essential.

- **Spanners** – As an electrician, the sizes you'll most probably use are 10mm, 13mm and 17mm, but it wouldn't hurt to get a full set if cost isn't an issue. Typical bolt and fixing sizes relate to these for supplementary bonding or affixing channel. Another suggestion would be to get a ratchet equivalent to save your arms!

Many of these can be argued in or out of an initial tool bag, depending on the typical days' work you're completing. It's always worth shopping around for the latest deals and *don't* necessarily get fixated on buying the latest brand or following the latest trend.

Colleges

If there's a summary statement to be made about colleges, it would be this as an obvious starting point: they're under-staffed, underfunded and under-equipped to deal with the spectrum of works that an apprentice electrician can complete as part of their daily life.

Now this may sound like an indictment of colleges and the further education system, and it is to some degree; however, there are many people in the education sector who really care about providing well-rounded, adequately funded education. Those of us who end up being educated by these establishments and people are the lucky few (you'll know who you are).

Most apprentices will enter the industry via the domestic sector. As simple examples, they won't encounter circuit protective devices such as air circuit breakers (ACB), moulded case circuit breakers (MCCB) and beyond. Colleges simply don't have these at their disposal. Most will have a practical workshop, with booths for completing practical examinations, using equipment and materials that have been terminated and utilised many times, so they're way beyond any guarantee from a manufacturer.

A key aspect is to ensure that, for you as a learner (and this can apply at any stage in your career, whether you're learning in year one of an apprenticeship course or week three of a six-week short course for inspection and testing), aiming simply to pass the test isn't the key to understanding the material you're being presented with. Within your working day, implementing, discussing and reviewing the information provided in a training course is an absolute must. This is achieved only with time. It's why the industry is so readily associated with the phrase "time-served apprentice".

There's such a quantity of information that's condensed into your time in college. Typically, for a day-release student, there will be distinct sessions in your educational day: scientific theory, practical, regulations and design.

Whilst some would say qualifications have got easier over the years, this isn't a reflection on colleges. Certification bodies such as City & Guilds and EAL set the standards for these exams. When exams have a pass mark of 50%, queries need to be raised about the standard of education.

As mentioned earlier, tutors are commonly underpaid. As a society, this is true for teachers across the nation. We expect these people to be the most knowledgeable about their subject area, good communicators, experienced and inspirational. If salaries are low, whilst this might attract a small number of incredibly talented and caring individuals who love to teach, it won't attract the best that industry has to offer. Until this is acknowledged and addressed, the education sector will always be last on the list of those who innovate and lead the electrical sector.

A full apprenticeship can cost in the region of £18,000 to deliver. If you're aged under 18, then there's no cost to either yourself or the employer. If you're aged 19 or older, you may incur a fee that's a small percentage of the costs over the four years.

You can go directly to businesses who may already be linked to local colleges, but it's always worth exploring your options. Many apprentices will opt to complete their apprenticeship with JTL, which is a non-profit organisation that teams up with employers to provide apprenticeships in the electrical sector; it was founded by the Electrical Contractors' Association (ECA) and Unite (the union, which we'll get on to in the "Trade Unions" section in *Chapter 10*).

Whilst many will think of it as a last resort in education, becoming an electrician still requires minimum qualifications for entry into apprenticeships. You need to have achieved GCSE level 2 qualifications (which is equivalent to the old grade C) in maths and English. If you don't hold these, many colleges will also offer them alongside the other parts of the curriculum, but just in case this worries you, it's a worst-case scenario that this needs to be achieved before the end-point assessment of your apprenticeship in year four.

End Point

After four years – assuming you've managed to navigate your way through the various assessments, exams and employment – the final step will be to undertake an end-point assessment, otherwise known as the Achievement Measurement 2 (AM2). The AM2 is broken down into key sections for assessment: safe isolation, installation, inspection, testing and certification, fault-finding, and assessment of applied knowledge. It's a five-day exam during which all these aspects/skills are evaluated. It's the most thorough examination you'll go through during the entire four-year apprenticeship.

There are many assessment centres up and down the country, so it's always worth reviewing the one that's nearest to you geographically. Many apprentices must stay away in hotels for the duration of their exam. Getting a spot in an exam can also be troublesome, as dates are usually fully packed due to a limited number of assessments being able to be completed in any given week.

Whilst this can seem daunting, you'll get tips and tricks along the way, which will make the mountain seem more like a molehill. One of the typical key tips given is to write down all results found when testing, including those not required by the certification documentation (for example, the short-circuit current across all phases), thus allowing all results to be reviewed and ensuring any anomalous readings to be captured and identified.

If – and it's a big if – you achieve all these qualifications (statistics show that almost 50% of those who start the journey won't qualify[4]), what awaits you is a career that will require constant development and expanding your expertise through a variety of qualifications. If there's a specialism, there's a qualification associated with it. Whether it's on working within hazardous areas or various specific industries, such as rail or even manufacturing, taking qualifications doesn't stop after you've initially become qualified.

This industry is littered with many educational establishments such as academies, colleges and further education centres – there are many names for them. What if one such establishment was openly advertising that you could achieve four years' worth of training and education in six weeks? You'd think you were dreaming...

CHAPTER 2

LATE ENTRANTS

Are Short Courses Good?

Some businesses within the electrical industry believe it's possible to condense what would typically be 200-plus weeks of an educational journey into the meagre amount of just six weeks.

No, you didn't just misread that.

For some time now, the electrical industry has been littered with educational businesses who deliver on this promise. They'll provide you with the necessary training and education to become a "fully qualified" electrician and be out in the world, earning the wages of a qualified electrician, just six weeks after starting their course.

It has provided many benefits for countless people over the years, and it's not for me to state whether it does or doesn't work for an individual. However, it needs to be clear that, whilst anyone can walk off the street and undertake multiple-choice exams, they can't be deemed immediately competent.

"Competence" is an important word within the electrical industry. Whether you're a qualified supervisor for a multinational business operating with hundreds of employees for a competent person scheme or simply managing your own installations as a self-employed electrician, both need you to be *equally* competent.

"Competence" is defined within Regulation 16 of The Electricity at Work Regulations 1989 as "a person having the appropriate technical knowledge, skills and experience to prevent danger or injury."[5] With everything that was discussed in *Chapter 1*, how can we expect an individual to comprehend fully what's legally expected of them under The Electricity at Work Regulations 1989 without giving them sufficient time to do so?

Imagine the worst: a tragedy has happened. A death has occurred from an electrical fault on a socket circuit. After just six weeks' training, the person in charge of the electrical works for the property was you. You're in the dock, charged as part of criminal proceedings. You're asked to "prove that you took all reasonable steps and exercised all due diligence to avoid the commission of that offence"[6] in line with The Electricity at Work Regulations 1989. How can someone know what they don't know? Well, in essence, that's competence: *knowing what you don't know.*

Now this example might be a worst-case scenario, but it isn't outside of the realms of possibility. When cutting over 8,000 hours of training down to just 240, then who's fooling whom?

With what I've just detailed, you might be thinking, *How's this shortened training allowed?* Well, the infrastructure enabling these types of courses is slowly being dulled. However, technical loopholes within the industry have facilitated the existence of short courses.

The entrants to these courses will undertake the same exams and leave with the same qualifications as those who take four years to achieve it. So what's the difference? The answer is purely the time to get the experience and exposure to the scenarios, installations and methodologies to become a suitably qualified and experienced electrical engineer.

The same people who undertake these courses can also, upon leaving, register to create a limited company; nothing prevents anyone from doing this unless they've recently filed for bankruptcy.

Since September 2021, the National Inspection Council for Electrical Installation Contracting (NICEIC) have removed the ability for those entering the industry in this manner to become approved members. However, there's nothing to stop someone operating in this manner and issuing their certification directly to the local authority. We'll touch on the various certification scenarios in *Chapter 10*.

We all just want something better for ourselves and our families, but it's important to educate those who take this route to make sure they understand the flaws.

However, it's also crucial to recognise when a shorter form of education is beneficial. Once a foundation of learning has been achieved, most electricians will typically continue their educational development journey through various forms of short courses. In this way, they'll be supplementing their knowledge as they learn new skills.

The fundamental one for electricians – the standard practice route of entry – is to undertake qualifications associated with inspection and testing, moving towards gaining the status of being an "approved" electrician. This has always been a bit of a misnomer as the qualification doesn't make you any more approved in the eyes of industry; rather, it's a term that simply separates an installation electrician from one who can inspect and test installations.

The term "approved" has been good and bad for industry. It has become a benchmark for electricians who want to be suitably trained in inspecting and testing installations. It has also created confusion for those external to the industry. The statement "If he isn't approved, he can't work on my property!" has resulted in many a project being awarded to an alternative electrical contractor.

> The fundamental point is that not all short courses are bad. Once you've qualified, many courses can be used to boost your journey and promote you within the industry. When committing to your working life as an electrician, you'll often hear "Every day is a school day." There will never be a truer statement.

Wages

As you can see, there are lots of variables to consider when entering the electrical industry. We must *always* be careful to not blame the person who undertakes a short course with the aim of becoming a qualified electrician. Whether it's unhappiness in their current job/role, poor wages or career prospects, each reason is just as a valid as the one before it.

One of the major issues that drives people to decide to take a short course is the salary.

There's a misapprehension regarding the wage an electrician earns. Since 2012, the minimum wage for an electrician has been floating around the £30,000 mark. This is based on the Joint Industry Board's (JIB's) annual determination, which sets out the minimum rates for its members. This is widely used as a base rate for companies throughout the industry, though most aren't actually members. It's a yardstick and a reasonable way of determining how you compare nationally with your own and/ or your company's wages.

To put this rough salary bracket into context, this is 50% higher than the current national minimum wage, which has been sitting at approximately £20,000 over the same period.

Now, if you were to be told that, in just six weeks' time, you could be earning 50% more than you are now, what struggling person or family isn't going to seriously consider it?

However, the truth is that apprentices aren't the best paid. Whilst the legal minimum wages are adhered to throughout the construction industry (noting there may still be some exceptions out there), it's typically adults who are the latecomers to the sector. The price of being an adult is that it's likely you'll come to the job with all the adult responsibilities: the mortgage, the bills and the family to support. It's those of us who can't afford the change of career late in the day who want to expedite the process as much as possible, *and who wouldn't?*

Finding employment as an adult learner with higher pay expectations is always going to be a challenge. But if we put ourselves into the shoes of the employer, under 18s are given more government-backed funding. So immediately, employing someone under that age is literally paying for itself.

If you started reading this book to discover the wealth associated with being an electrician, then unfortunately for you, the myth of high salaries for electricians is exactly that: a myth. There might be adverts for jobs in national or even local newspapers offering way in excess of this; there might be companies operating in central London offering £100,000. But they don't tell you that it requires working a minimum of 12 hours a day, seven days a week to earn anywhere near that figure. It's always vital to read the small print. If something seems too good to be true, then it usually is.

This, alongside national media stories and social media posts, acts to distort the public's perception when hiring a tradesperson. Even amongst trades, the perception is that the electrician is the one earning the big bucks. Statistically, this simply isn't true. Thanks to programmes on television where rogue traders are caught operating, it has furthered the belief that all tradesmen are *on the take* in some way or another – which, again, just simply isn't true.

Fundamentally, every entrant into the electrical industry should be aware that, whether you complete the formal education part of your training in six weeks or four years, the journey is always ongoing and the learning never stops.

One thing we do as teenagers that we don't do as adults is undertake work experience. If you're unhappy in your career, take a week's holiday, offer your services for free to a business and work with them for a week. Find out if a career in the electrical industry is for you. It might be the best thing you ever do.

The Job Market

The job market is a competitive place. The skills gap is ever increasing. Those within an ageing workforce are retiring, and their skills and knowledge aren't being replaced. Fewer small businesses are willing to take the financial risk associated with employing staff, particularly unqualified staff in the form of apprentices.

Something that's underestimated by those outside the construction industry is the type of employment used in a construction project's workforce. Large-scale commercial and industrial projects predominantly utilise agency labour. Achieving a project's goals through short-term staff is common all over the country, but not more so than in the bustling metropolis of London, where buildings are being erected every day. This impacts a person's ability to find available companies who are willing to commit to training new entrants.

Agency work is the alternative to permanent employment. This is most likely the way the majority of those who can't find a permanent employer will find work within the industry. There are many pros and cons to gaining employment in this manner. A major con is the lack of a mentor to guide you through your time, who has that oversight in understanding what skills you lack and addressing them through your working week, over many years. An adult learner might be able to appreciate this and address it by asking the right questions. Unfortunately, most young adults don't. Some may find a mentor on a project-by-project basis. However, this isn't guaranteed, and the expectation to make yourself value for money may lead to being quickly removed if the overall benefit of employing you doesn't favour the construction project.

Over the last couple of decades, more teenagers have been choosing to stay in education on completing their GCSEs, electing to progress into further education via taking A levels rather than entering the world of work via an apprenticeship. This has now been reinforced by the government's legislative changes that require young people to stay in education or training until they they're 18. This has led to a further deficit in the workforce. Many have echoed the concerns associated with this, which have been raised up to and including the government level.

There's an argument that the current education system doesn't help each student progress towards selecting their career. There's a lack of support for students in terms of finding their passions, interests, likes and dislikes – alongside determining what their skills are. However, the purpose of a well-functioning education system should be to determine how each person can utilise their skills to not only be a benefit to society but to provide them with some level of job satisfaction or even purpose.

Those who work within the practical workshops and classrooms won't necessarily find the routes into industry without suitable career guidance being provided prior to reaching GCSE level. Those who do find their way into the trades will typically find this route through their paternal mentors: family businesses and skills passed down generation to generation.

Ultimately, many people won't find what they're good at or enjoy until later in life. This is the very antithesis of what the electrical industry is experiencing currently, and it's a situation that isn't showing any immediate signs of stopping.

There's an age-old saying that's frequently spoken but rarely heard: "If you enjoy your work, you'll never work a day in your life." You'll struggle find anyone in any walk of life who won't agree with this statement, including the electrical industry.

The Skills Gap

This is something that may have always been present since the Industrial Revolution. Have there always been enough engineers to go around? It's something that has long been tangibly visible to those within the engineering sectors. It's certainly evident to those who are at the start of the engineering journey on seeing their classmates withdraw from the lengthy process.

If you've undertaken a degree or an apprenticeship, you'll have felt and seen the class size shrink, with people falling by the wayside who started on this ambitious four-year journey with you. It's natural for this to happen on all educational career paths, so this isn't a phenomenon that's isolated within the electrical industry.

There are those, though, who deny that an ever-widening gap in the lack of available, trained, qualified engineers even exists. The framing of statistics also doesn't help. They aren't visibly trended over time, with successive governments wanting to highlight the improvements being made under their own party's stewardship.

In the academic year of 2021/22, 740,000 people participated in an apprenticeship in England.[7] Of those, 349,000 were starting and 137,000 were finishing.[8] There are two ways to interpret this information. We could say, "Wow! England has managed to increase the apprenticeship uptake by 250% compared with four years ago." The figures quoted for numbers of apprentices are typically those from the start rather than the tail-end of apprenticeships.

The alternative narrative is that, realistically, 212,000 apprentices won't make it to the end of the course; that's 39%. When considering these figures within an overall figure of 740,000 apprentices, it does create a false vision or an illusion that simply isn't being reflected in industry.

If we compare the 137,000 apprentices who are finishing their courses to previous years, we see the statistics from the 2020/21 academic year show that this number has decreased by 12% from 156,000, and there's an even greater fall since 2018/19 when it was 185,000.[9] This demonstrates a total falling trend of 26% in four years.

This isn't the only factor impacting the skills gap. An ageing workforce is also playing its part in extending the skills gap. The average age of an engineer in the UK is 55. In the next 10–15 years, many of these people will be retiring. Is there enough time for their knowledge to be passed on to the next generation before this huge part of the industry and the workforce is lost?

As an apprentice, you may also experience job protection from the older generations. Many willingly share their knowledge, but some are acutely aware of their job security, and retaining the knowledge means keeping their job.

More and more people are noting the skills gap and committing time to improving future generations and trying to inspire them, not only to enter the electrical industry but also to stay in it!

We're also seeing job adverts remaining open for longer periods of time. The wages for specialist skill sets and experience are increasing. So is there a better time to become an electrical engineer?

CHAPTER 3

QUALIFYING

The Moment After

One of the best feelings in the world is when you reach the milestone of qualifying and being able to call yourself an electrician. Suddenly, you've gained a newfound freedom that you didn't have as an apprentice only 24 hours earlier. The world has a new respect for you that it didn't before. You're now a qualified spark!

Unfortunately, all isn't what it seems – although it is a good feeling! The respect you've earned will be the result of your employer, mentors and peers reviewing your work and tracking your progress over the last four years. You won't suddenly have freedom, as responsibility was already being delegated to you, incrementally and more prominently, not only in your final year but also throughout your whole journey as an apprentice.

There's a truth in there, though. You do walk through the metaphorical door to becoming a qualified electrician.

The first major step is to run your own job or, if it's part of some bigger project, to take control of an area. This can be from something as simple as changing some sockets to installing a building management system (BMS) in a plantroom, depending on the scope of work completed by you and your employer. Hopefully, if you've been fortunate enough to complete your apprenticeship with the same employer, they'll have developed you according to their business needs, which will result in a minimal shock to the system when this stage of your career finally arrives. It's all in the planning.

Abruptly, all the responsibility lies with you: finding the address of the place of work; refilling your van with fuel to get there; setting off early to make sure you're on time; checking the scope of work and visiting a local wholesaler to get any necessary materials; wearing a smart, presentable uniform; liaising with customers in a polite manner; ensuring any risk assessments and method statements are signed and followed, whilst ensuring your client's and your own safety at all times; and completing any safe isolations required. The list is almost endless.

Then there's the tricky business of actually completing the installation. You'll be working around the needs of the customer, who can't have the power off, can't have too much noise, etc. All whilst delivering to the programme to make certain the business survives and makes at least a minimal profit to return the overhead that you, as an apprentice, have been for the previous four years.

Upon completing the installation works, you'll need to test it and fill in all necessary documentation and certification, which is to be reviewed and verified by the company's qualified supervisor for any one of the competent person schemes. These are the sink-or-swim skills you'll be required to learn rapidly. Documentation can seem like a minefield when you're first starting to complete it. As you'll no doubt be wanting to impress those who'll review it, it's always a challenge. Making mistakes is OK – you just need to make sure you learn from them.

Next comes the arduous task of tidying, hoovering and putting everything back you removed to complete the works, with the idea being to make it look like you were never there.

Finally, you'll need to get back to the office, sitting in traffic all the while, only to return way beyond your contracted working hours; you'll hand in your paperwork whilst picking up tomorrow's documentation to begin the process all over again.

It can seem like a lot of responsibility and be very daunting, but not all jobs are like this.

It may seem a repetitive job to do day by day. However, even in the most domestic of settings, there's always something new for an electrician to learn. That could be fault-finding, installing new equipment or simply finding a tool that completes wall chases for you with one-tenth of the dust exposure. There's a saying in the industry that "You never do the same job twice."

The next step is going on to larger installations and projects. This is where a new skill set needs to come into play. Whether you progress into managing others, teams, subcontractors, commercial issues or safety, there are many other skill sets to be learned for your upward progression.

One thing's for sure: you'll forever be able to point a variety of properties and buildings and say, "I worked on that," for many years to come.

Other Qualifications

Since the dawn of the electrical industry, safety has come to play a bigger and bigger role in it. The eventual reduction of annual deaths from approximately 275 per year in the 1960s down to 40 in 2020 showcases the progress the construction industry has made.[10]

The introduction of a variety of legislation – including the Health and Safety at Work Act 1974 and The Electricity at Work Regulations 1989, to name but two – has helped push the agenda of safety forward for the everyday working electrician.

With this increased agenda for ensuring everyone makes it home at the end of the working day came a fundamental requirement to increase the safety training everyone receives.

To work on a construction site as an electrician, you will – as a minimum – be expected to have passed the Joint Industry Board Electrotechnical Certification Scheme (JIB ECS), for which you'll receive your ECS card. Whilst it isn't a qualification as such, it's a multiple-choice exam with a high pass mark for basic construction-site-safety competence (we'll discuss this further in *Chapter 10*).

Working at height is a common risk for electricians; lighting is typically always at a high level, particularly in commercial and industrial settings. Installations include lighting columns, high bay lighting and many other types of lighting. These will typically require access equipment of some sort, which can be self-constructed in the form of access towers.

In this instance, you'd look to undertake the Prefabricated Access Suppliers' and Manufacturers' Association (PASMA) training. This will educate you on how to erect and inspect access towers and podiums, amongst other things. These aren't the most flexible means of providing access at height, particularly as an electrician will be wanting to move around an installation, light to light.

Where manoeuvring and flexibility is required, you might look at training associated with the International Powered Access Federation (IPAF). This is for your powered access; that is, your drivable equipment. All working-at-height training should typically come with detail regarding working with harnesses, and none more so than powered access. The potential to be thrown from the vehicle is the biggest risk associated with operating this heavy-duty equipment. There will be many names for these throughout the industry, including scissor lifts and mobile elevated working platforms (MEWPs). Familiarity is key, particularly in commercial installations.

Both the IPAF and PASMA qualifications come with neat cards, which will slot into any wallet alongside your ECS card for ease of use.

EVs have recently evolved their own subset of qualifications. There has been rapid change within the EV sector. Qualifications have already come and gone. Whilst we have the relatively new City & Guilds 2919 qualification, updates will come as the technology advances at a rapid pace. The electrical industry had remained stagnant for many years with regards to technology. It's now struggling to keep up! EVs are certainly a current trend, but whether they'll stand the test of time remains to be seen. However, obtaining these qualifications alongside ones for solar power and battery storage will strongly align you with economic trends for green energy in the domestic setting, introducing your skill set to a rapidly growing market.

The main qualification that sits outside the standard apprenticeship qualifications is an obvious one: the regulations! This is a qualification that, at its heart, requires a fundamental understanding of the dos and don'ts within electrical installations. It's an open-book exam, with multiple-choice answers and a pass mark of 60%. All sound easy? Well, many won't leave with a pass. A sufficient understanding of the book is required in advance of taking any such exam.

There are many other qualifications to take as an electrician as you expand into a variety of specialisms. From emergency lighting to portable appliance testing (PAT), these may be useful additional strings to your bow. However, one such course that can be undertaken post qualifying as an electrician is the City & Guilds 2396 electrical design course. This course gives a greater in-depth understanding of electrical design. It's assessed via several exams and a coursework project (something that's rare in the world of electrical qualifications). These courses are typically delivered over several weeks and are also considered to be a short course.

After completing the design qualification, many within the electrical industry may choose to go on to further education in the form of a Higher National Certificate (HNC) or Higher National Diploma (HND) qualification, although there's no requisite to do so. The HNC and HND are courses that parallel the content of university years one and two, respectively, so a degree is viable once they've been completed. These courses are delivered through a variety of coursework and projects in an array of selectable study areas, such as mathematics, mechanical engineering, control systems and other engineering sciences. These aren't cheap qualifications and typically require at least two years' effort each, usually on day release with a local education establishment. These show you have a commitment to developing yourself and investing in your career.

Supervising Others

The job can be tricky enough to complete without having to look after, or think about, someone else's needs. Well, this is the life of a supervisor, which is the next step post completing an apprenticeship.

Supervising requires a different set of skills to being an installer. It's the first step into the world of management. You might be simply supervising an apprentice or, potentially, as much as a team of 20 operating on a multimillion-pound project. In either instance, the skill set remains the same.

Both written and verbal communication are the cornerstones of this skill set. You need to be able to communicate adequately – not just clearly and concisely but also technically. When coordinating with colleagues, clients or other contractors, it's fundamental. Written communication can also be safety critical. This might be communicating at a safety briefing, reviewing a method statement or conducting a point-of-work risk assessment; these are all things worth due consideration before simply cracking on with the day's work.

A subset of communication is having good interpersonal skills. Being technically able to communicate is one thing, but understanding someone's personal situation is another. Everyone is an individual and has their own specific needs or requirements. This can range from the petty to the serious.

Having the ability to ensure everyone feels heard is as important as any technical capability a supervisor may have.

Decision-making is a difficult skill to master. This can be based on technical knowledge, but experience is equally valid. With experience comes the ability to not only understand the requirements of the installation but also to have an understanding of contractual requirements, the programme, commercial impacts and many more. These must all enter the mind of a supervisor.

You must use critical thinking to weigh up options and predict the best possible outcomes, not only for the customer but also, more importantly, for the business you work for. Sometimes, the decision will mean one of those won't get the best possible outcome. Justifying these decisions to your superiors or clients can be nerve-racking, but it's a necessary evil. Consulting others who may be more experienced is invaluable, especially when you're relatively inexperienced. This may be a pride-swallowing act, but it will ultimately be a fruitful one.

> Time management is important. Everything must be done on schedule and delivered to budget. Prioritising and delegating tasks is one aspect of time management that's often forgotten. You can't achieve everything on your own, so remembering to delegate and use the support of your team is key to prioritising your time.

The ability to manage conflict resolution when difficulties arise can also be a useful tool to rely on. This can range from issues between colleagues to dealing with unreasonable demands from a client. The skill of compromising is vital to keeping a project moving forwards and managing a team. This isn't a self-help book, and I'm sure there are many good sources of information on this if you wish to look. It's merely a fact that to manage other people, of all skill levels and abilities, you must be a good communicator.

Mentoring, particularly when you're operating within smaller-scale businesses, can be a lifeline to the success of that business in the long term. Investing your time in people can develop their skills far quicker than expecting it all to run smoothly with a pick-it-up-as-you-go attitude.

Remaining positive is also a very useful soft skill that many don't always recognise. Alongside optimism, this is pushing to complete a task or project when the going gets tough and being able to find that extra something that enables you to convey to team members or even customers that all has gone well when, in truth, it has been a struggle. When fighting against runaway budgets or projects over-running against the programme, staying positive in those moments when it's not going well will help give the project and/or business that extra chance of long-term success.

As well as all the soft skills we've discussed, there are also some formal qualifications that can be undertaken. The Site Supervisor Safety Training Scheme (SSSTS) and the Site Manager Safety Training Scheme (SMSTS) are two such courses that are direct routes to becoming a supervisor. These courses will typically test your underpinning knowledge surrounding safety for the people you're responsible for. The Health and Safety at Work Act 1974 is a key part of this, as it fundamentally tries to get the students to leave the course with a change in their mindset towards behavioural safety, ultimately changing the culture on worksites throughout the country.

The other primary qualification to undertake is a first aid course. Your goal as a supervisor is for everyone to go home at the end of the day. Accidents can and do happen, particularly on construction sites, where buildings are incomplete, heavy-duty tools are in use, scaffolding is in place, etc. Even on perfectly well-run construction sites, human error can occur at any time, so ensuring you're prepared could save lives.

You can consider other health-and-safety-related courses or even management courses too. There are also many routes away from the tools and into an office chair. Many of these skills can be practised in one way or another by everyone, including apprentices.

CHAPTER 4

INSPECTION AND TESTING

The Qualification

The other main qualification outside an apprenticeship to become a working electrician is for inspection and testing. This seems like an obvious one to discuss when thinking about an electrician's daily work. However, as discussed previously, the industry's approach to training, qualifications and the ability to complete the work can appear disjointed and unclear to those outside it.

Having completed an apprenticeship, it's reasonable to expect that multiple modules of such a course would include the ability to inspect and test the work any electrician completes. Well, this is correct to a certain degree. Modules are taught and verified as part of the standard apprenticeship model under City & Guilds 2330 (or equivalent), and these do qualify an electrician under a competent person scheme to self-certify. The apprenticeship journey, whilst including these elements, will require you to gain experience during your working week with an employer. It's important to remember to not to pick up any of your employer's bad habits (assuming you can spot them!).

It's recommended within the industry that, once you've completed your apprenticeship, you spend sufficient time to gain the necessary skills to then undertake the inspection and testing qualification. Many state that two years is required. However, many others won't have followed this guidance and instead complete it within this timeframe.

The qualifications have changed multiple times in recent years, creating aspects of confusion even for electricians themselves. For many years, the inspection and testing qualification was City & Guilds 2391. It has subsequently reverted to this qualification, but it had temporarily been broken into two sections: City & Guilds 2394, the initial verification qualification, which enabled someone to inspect and test their own installation; and City & Guilds 2395, covering periodic inspection and testing, which enabled an electrician to sign off others' work via electrical installation certificates and to review existing installations via the electrical installation condition reporting process.

Having now reverted to the 2391 qualification, many consider the latest iteration of the exam to be not as stringent as its original predecessor in terms of its ability to fail a student. However, it's one of the few written exams an electrician will face. This, in addition to both a multiple-choice and a practical exam, makes passing it no mean feat.

The specific topics covered in the City & Guilds 2391 course may vary, depending on the training provider and the course version, but it typically includes the following key areas:

- **Electrical inspection procedures** – Understanding the procedures and requirements for conducting thorough electrical inspections of domestic, commercial and industrial installations.

- **Electrical testing methods** – Learning various electrical testing techniques, including continuity testing, insulation resistance testing, earth fault loop impedance testing and more.

- **Requirements of British Standard (BS) 7671** – Becoming familiar with the British Standard for Electrical Installations (BS 7671) and its latest regulations.

- **Safe isolation procedures** – Ensuring safety when working with live electrical systems, through proper isolation procedures and using lock-out and tag-out techniques.

- **Completion of electrical certification** – Learning how to complete electrical certificates and reports accurately, detailing the findings of inspections and testing.

- **Fault diagnosis and rectification** – Identifying and diagnosing faults in electrical installations and determining the appropriate remedial actions.

- **Practical assessment** – Undertaking practical assessments in which candidates demonstrate their competence in inspection and testing tasks.

Assuming you hold all the other relevant qualifications, adding this qualification will facilitate the word "approved" being added to your JIB ECS gold card. This qualification is viewed as valuable, particularly when employers are hiring. It doesn't mean someone who doesn't hold this qualification can't test and someone who does can, but for a business deferring activities to trained and competent people, it's in everyone's interests to hold a qualification that demonstrates your skill set.

There are short-course options to condense the learning time into one to two weeks; however, it's preferable to stretch these over many weeks to give sufficient opportunity for acquiring the skills in the intervening period between lessons.

Having said that, everyone will learn in a different way. There's no right or wrong way to achieve this.

Test Kits

Many find inspecting and testing a daunting prospect at the beginning of their career. Like with anything, it's a skill that can soon be learned – particularly when completing electrical installation condition reports (formerly known as "periodic inspections") on a regular basis.

The width and breadth of the visual inspections an electrician might find is a book in its own right. All observations are detailed in a written report. Some electricians who are making use of software or a tablet to complete their inspection reports will add photographic evidence to support the visual observations made. This can be a useful tool for the next electrician or supervisor who encounters the work, as it may not always be you who comes back to fix an issue. Photographic evidence also helps sceptical clients more easily justify the spend when rectifying the faults in future.

Historically, test kits for electricians included a variety of individual testers; for example, some electricians may remember the Robin series of test instruments. However, in modern times, as technology has improved, they've now typically been converted into single test units known as "multifunction testers". These testers have the ability to complete a range of different tests, including continuity, insulation resistance, earth loop impedance and residual current device (RCD) tests.

The instruments aren't cheap, and they also must be calibrated regularly. This is verified as part of the competent person assessments. Lots of wholesalers now offer open days to bring in test kits for calibration and have a bacon roll whilst you wait. Other than buying a vehicle, this is one of the largest expenses you'll have as an electrician; whilst calibration costs are typically reasonable, the initial outlay is slightly more problematic, with kits going up to and above the £1,000 mark.

There are several pieces of supplementary equipment required in any test kit. Voltage indicators and proving units are essential. Being able to verify live supplies is a fundamental requirement of your career as an electrician, even whilst you're an apprentice. It must be taken seriously by *all*. Following the safe isolation procedure can mean the difference between life and death. Sadly, many have found this out to their detriment.

A safe isolation kit will go hand in hand with a voltage indicator and proving unit. This includes a variety of locking-off devices for circuit protection of all shapes and sizes. It's worth noting that different devices are required for different types of equipment; miniature circuit breakers (MCBs) won't utilise the same lock off as a door interlocked isolator or an MCCB. The final part of the kit is the ID tags. Clearly identifying the circuit(s) you've locked off is as valuable as the device itself. A danger notification will make people think twice. The name and contact number on it should be clear, and it should include a "Do not operate" label; this should direct them to you without incident.

Many electricians will also carry socket fault-finders. These can save massive amounts of time, and again, the technology is ever increasing. Historically, they showed the polarity of terminations without you needing to remove a socket face plate physically. Now they can show fault conditions down to where the fault resides, and they're even able to indicate voltage and earth loop impedance ranges. These aren't to be solely relied upon, but they're another string to your bow.

Over time, you might find the extra funds to add items to your test kit. For example, clamp meters and thermal-imaging cameras are great additional extras that allow you to explore the operation of an installation; in particular, they give you a greater understanding of issues such as diverted neutral currents and phenolic degradation.

Whilst multifunction test kits aren't an immediate concern when you're an apprentice, the priority should be to invest in a safe isolation kit with all the required accessories.

Codebreaking

Inspecting an electrical installation is something that's more nuanced and takes time to learn. Interpretation can also be a serious part of the discussion here. Whilst you might feel the regulations are something that shouldn't be challenged, a lot is left to engineering judgement. No two installations are the same. Every installation will require its own assessment and design, and it will have its own user requirements.

We may have an ideal image of what we think the regulations should be. Some think of them as the maximum to be done, and others think of them as the minimum requirement for an installation. This can vastly alter the quality and compliance. How compliant will the installation be in years to come? Or even months?

One such example is the reintroduction of metal-clad consumer units under amendment three of the 17th edition of BS 7671 in 2016. As with all changes in regulations, they're phased in to avoid the panic and chaos of sudden non-compliance being thrown at households throughout the country. The introduction of the aforementioned change was finally implemented after six months on 1st January 2016. However, a consumer unit replacement completed in December 2015 may well have been utilising a plastic enclosure; yet one month later, if an electrical installation condition report were to be completed, a C3 non-compliance to BS 7671 would be noted or potentially even a C2, depending on other variables.

You might be unfamiliar with the grading system associated with observations, so let me explain. We have the C3, as stated previously, which specifies that improvement is recommended. This doesn't require any urgent attention, unlike C2 and C1, which denote potentially dangerous and danger is present, respectively.

Not all issues will be able to be found within the time allowed for an electrical installation condition report. Unless you're fortunate enough to have a customer who'll simply cover the hourly rate for as long as it takes to get it right, you may only get a few hours to a day to do the review and complete the documentation.

If a fault is known but can't be clearly detailed – for example, if it's a fault hidden within the fabric of the building – then further investigation may be required.

It should be noted that in all cases of grades C1 or C2 and further investigation, nothing more than a report stating it's unsatisfactory can be provided to the person ordering the work. This forces them to undertake the necessary action to close out the issues. Some electricians may make use of danger notifications as a way to emphasise the issue. Danger notifications don't have any relation to BS 7671, but they're a useful way of highlighting immediate issues.

It's important to remember that, as an electrician, you shouldn't walk away from a C1 or C2 observation without taking reasonable action. If that action is isolating the issue as a bare minimum and removing the issue / making it safe without considerable costs being incurred, it's the responsible solution.

Some of the other verifications you'll complete as part of a visual inspection are confirming conductor sizes, rating protective devices in relation to conductor sizes, and coordinating between both size and rating. These are just a few examples, but it's important to remember that you'll also use all your senses. Whether you're listening for arcing or other issues, or smelling any burning terminations, all your senses must be deployed when completing inspections.

Deciphering which observational code you should attribute to any given issue is very much down to the individual. There are some useful resources out there to use on your learning journey. The competent person scheme National Association of Professional Inspectors and Testers (NAPIT) has produced a book called *NAPIT EICR* [Electrical Installation Condition

Reports] *Codebreakers*, which gives lots of examples and guidance to assist with interpreting regulations.[11] Many disagree with some of the content of the guide, but it's just that – a guide and a foundation to build on.

Testing

Testing consists of the multitude of tests necessary to complete electrical certification and documentation in accordance with BS 7671. There are many stages of testing to learn: the continuity of conductors, ring final continuity of conductors, insulation resistance, polarity dead and live, earth loop impedance and RCD testing. All these are designed to test the cabling installation and protective devices.

There are many tips and tricks to learn along the way on how to assess test results. Unfortunately, not everyone will know them. It's anticipated that, if you're a qualified supervisor for a competent person scheme, many of these skills for assessing test certification will be at your disposal.

Here's a quick detailed example of using calculations to verify results:

Ze + (r1+r2) = Zs

Where the origin earth loop impedance value (Ze) plus the continuity resistance value (r1+r2) will equal the end of line earth loop impedance (Zs) test result.

A common trick employed by many who complete either the dead or live test alone is to manufacture the other results using this calculation. Whilst there are times when it's acceptable to use this calculation, as there might be a restriction on your ability to test, any restrictions should be noted as a limitation within a condition report. However, employing this method for all circuit test results is immediately obvious to any reviewer.

No installation is perfect, and it certainly won't align with any calculations. The real-world imperfections of resistance increases in load, terminations, etc. will affect these readings. If the prior calculation is utilised as a tool for verifying the actual results, this can facilitate you identifying observations or concerns.

Damaging equipment is another part of the inspection work that can be frustrating. After taking an installation apart, it may not want to go back together. Electrical sins can be hidden, and once they've been discovered, they can be a nightmare. Conductors that have been cut short and cross-threaded screws, to name but a few, are the bane of every electrician's day. Not to mention the risks associated with testing. Insulation resistance is the one test in which a higher than usual voltage is injected to detect deterioration in conductor insulation. This can be a test voltage of up to 1,000V, so it's important to remember not all electronics in the home enjoy being fried at this voltage range.

You'll now also need to verify the operation of devices other than RCDs, such as the arc fault detection and surge protection devices that are now beginning to be commonly installed in domestic consumer units. Whilst these units aren't currently testable using the typical electrician-owned multifunction tester, this is anticipated to be a future development.

All the books will come at a premium price; but within a year or two of commencing your apprenticeship, it will be incredibly worthwhile to purchase *Guidance Note 3: Inspection & Testing*.[12] Whilst these books are updated with each edition of the regulations, the basic practical elements remain the same.

As mentioned elsewhere in this book, the other book that will provide oversight of all aspects, including inspection and testing, is the *On-Site Guide*.[13] This book devotes less space to inspection and testing, but it captures the basics sufficiently well for you to commence the learning process as an apprentice.

CHAPTER 5

PICK A SECTOR

Domestic

Working in the domestic sector is effectively doing what it says on the tin: working in people's properties or homes. There's a perception amongst some in the industry that installations within a domestic setting might be easier than commercial or industrial installations. This simply isn't true. It requires a completely different skill set to those working in commercial or industrial sectors.

The work of an electrician in a domestic property is rarely seen. Most installations will reside behind the fabric of walls, be hidden in loft spaces or sit in the voids beneath floorboards. As an apprentice electrician, you'll spend time drilling joists and threading cables through tight spaces, including in lofts, to ensure these cables and installations remain seamless. You'll be chasing walls (hammering brickwork to provide cable channels) within compliant zones to facilitate cabling from ceilings to fixture positions. It's dusty work and usually completed by an apprentice. Such cabling work is known as the "first fix" of an installation.

Fitting sockets, pendants and spotlights is the bread-and-butter work for electricians in this sector of the trade. This uses twin and earth cabling (6242Y) of varying sizes throughout. It also includes wiring ring circuits for socket outlets plus wiring larger radial circuits for the heavier-load appliances in the home, such as an electric shower or cooker (I won't get started on the ring-versus-radial debate).

Installing all the fixtures and terminating the cables is known as the "second fix". For a complete rewire of a property, this might also include replacing the consumer unit and installing the latest protective devices, such as surge protection.

The domestic sector is expanding its vocabulary. With the introduction of EV chargers, solar panels and battery storage, it's becoming a complex minefield for the electricians who aren't necessarily familiar with the developments in technology. Additional training and professional development are required, alongside gaining experience to expand further into these fields.

Another aspect of this industry sector is that it can provide flexible working hours for those who are self-employed.

Call-outs are a common part of an electrician's day job, such as responding to clients who've lost lighting or power circuits. Fault-finding is a key aspect of this job. Developing inspection and testing skills in this area, alongside obtaining sufficient amounts of experience, is what can make a good fault-finder. These are all aspects that are captured as part of the end-point AM2 assessment discussed earlier.

If you're a contractor who only completes domestic installations, the industry does facilitate this with competent person schemes providing domestic installer registration. Apprentices are also now able to select the domestic electrician route specifically, which is designed around learning the skill set required. Many debate the validity of this qualification when compared to the standard apprenticeship route, which doesn't aim specifically at any industry sector, thus facilitating the ability to move between sectors at any point during your career.

Whatever your route into the domestic sector, it's an ever-expanding part of the electrical industry, with challenges ahead.

Commercial

Electrical installations within the commercial sector will vary from those in the domestic sector in many ways. Whilst commercial installations will utilise the methods described in the section on the domestic sector, such as concealing installations and cabling within building fabrics, the commercial sector will also show the cabling and cabling management systems, otherwise known as "containment".

Within office settings, flexibility is commonly required, so as to be able to rearrange furniture and move the positions of equipment. This is managed electrically via dado trunking systems. These consist of two or three compartments made of PVC. These are regularly installed around the perimeter of a room or office. With adjustable back boxes, they can facilitate the small power and data cabling required to run IT equipment within offices. For larger, more open-plan offices, you may find that the building uses suspended flooring. This can facilitate cabling installations, often using basket tray containment systems or cable matting. These will terminate into floor-mounted boxes, which is again to provide data and small power cabling to desks, typically supporting IT equipment.

Cabling within these systems generally tends to move away from the twin and earth cabling towards PVC singles (BS6491X). Consideration is needed to choose the appropriate option from various types of cables. There are low-smoke, zero-halogen equivalents to both twin and earth (BS6242B) and the PVC singles (BS6491B). These cables are made use of when considering the risks associated with fire, as they produce very little smoke and have reduced toxicity.

In commercial settings, you're more likely to encounter heating, ventilation and air conditioning (HVAC) systems. These may be controlled by a BMS. The control systems associated with these increase the complexity of commercial installations. They interface with fire alarm systems, security systems and many other systems to create an automated response and building control, even when reacting to just a temperature change within an area of the building.

These buildings will typically have plant rooms. They're usually located either close to the roof or in the basement, with electrical risers facilitating distribution to each floor. This is where we see an increased requirement to use circuits for a larger load, in which BS88-type fuses are necessary and low-voltage assemblies (LVAs) provide distribution (panels).

Cabling for these types of distribution systems will necessitate steel wire armoured cable. Whilst the domestic sector might employ this cable type infrequently, for things such as external supplies or garden lighting, this is often the cable type of choice in the commercial and industrial sectors. It provides mechanical protection in this riskier environment for cabling. This type of cabling will require glanding terminations with the steel wire trimmed and connected to the earthing system for the circuit. In some instances, this is instead of having a separate conductor.

Commercial installations will also consider the people working within the offices in the event of an emergency. Regularly maintaining the fire alarm systems and emergency lighting is the responsibility of the duty holder for that business. Covered by its own BS (BS 5266), this requires further training to achieve competence in this field, as do fire detection and alarm systems under BS 5839. Many installations will require ongoing servicing and maintenance. This can be a lucrative way of generating regular work amongst commercial clients.

Data systems are another aspect of electrical work, particularly in commercial settings, where Cat6 cables (only one amongst many types of cable) are installed throughout. Terminating and working with servers can be sensitive and time pressured. Where servers are employed, you might find an uninterruptable power supply (UPS). Commonly found alongside data storage, these can help ensure no data is lost during power failures. They support the equipment until a back-up generator is energised or the power supply is re-energised. The electrical complexity of generators requires much more thought. Controlling this interface can become an area of expertise.

There are other aspects of commercial work, including wiring temporary electrics for events. These must be completed in line with BS 7909, and this is again another area of expertise that can be expanded into. Whether it's festivals, exhibitions or events, these can certainly provide their own unique challenges.

Many new installations will require the designs to be reviewed and accepted in advance of any construction work beginning. They'll typically be managed by contracted scopes of delivery between different subcontractors. Usually, the scale is much greater than for domestic works, unless it's on the scale of a multimillion-pound new-build property or housing estate.

Electricians will be required on many levels to make certain that the correct documentation, supervision, design, risk assessment and method statements (amongst many other variables) are all in place to facilitate the work commencing.

In the commercial sector, much like the industrial sector, the site controls and access are clearly defined. Completion of the Construction Skills Certification Scheme (CSCS) or the equivalent is required; inductions and competence verification are day-to-day activities in these environments due to the nature of the work.

Industrial

Industrial electrical installations are another step further than the commercial installations detailed in the previous section. You may see larger cabling installations, distribution arrangements and even high-voltage installations sometimes, in which independent supplies are provided – although this is its own genre in the electrical world. This utilises the aforementioned steel or aluminium wire armoured cables, even replacing the copper conductor itself with aluminium. Containment for cabling installations such as these will most likely employ larger cable trays and ladder. Manufacturing channel bracketry (which electricians up and down the country commonly refer to by the brand name Unistrut) to provide containment and cabling support will be a learning curve for any industrial electrical apprentice during their formative years.

Not dissimilar to the control associated with commercial BMSs, control is an important aspect of industrial work. Typically, this will be the control of the process that's the next key stage. This could be controlling trains through signalling arrangements, controlling robotic machinery on a food manufacturing production line or managing a river level at a weir gate. The installations are endless, found in every corner of society and function in partnership with electricity.

The interface with mechanical equipment when controlling a process becomes much greater, whether that's pumps, motors, or other various plant or equipment of all shapes and sizes. Variable speed drives begin to come into play, alongside other types of motor starter selection.

Different installations will have different considerations. One factor that comes into play in the industrial sector is hazardous areas. Making everything gas/dust tight whilst limiting the potential release of energy in these installations is imperative for avoiding large explosions. For example, when you think of the complexity and nature of a petrol station, this is a hazardous area where members of the public interact with the installation. You have pumps, vehicles, lighting, controls and signalling all operating to provide this required service of refuelling your vehicle. This type of installation occurs throughout industries, manufacturing, utility systems and many more. Each requires a separate skill set, training and education.

The control cabling in these types of settings will still be the steel wire armoured cabling, with slight nuances to the structure of the internal core arrangements, such as using BS 5308 cabling. In some instances, screening the cabling with metal foil is required to prevent electromagnetic interference from other cables, occasionally even the individual screening of cores is needed to prevent "crosstalk" between other cores contained within the same cable. This is but one example of a multitude of control cabling applications.

One cable that regularly encroaches its way back into the commercial and domestic markets is SY cabling, which is a braided steel cable with a transparent PVC outer sheath. This is commonly utilised for control systems, potentially those in manufacturing settings with machinery operating in parallel to controls. However, it's frequently utilised in domestic installations, particularly externally, and treated like a standard steel wire armoured cable. Many have installed it outside, not considering its poor ultraviolet (UV) resistant properties will make it begin to crack and cause nuisance tripping faults a few years after its installation.

Industrially, it's to be expected that, when working in a factory setting where heavy machinery will be involved, manufacturers like to have the ability to move plant and equipment around to change their production lines to suit their business needs. Similarly to how dado trunking is used in a commercial office setting, electrical flexibility is created by employing high-level busbar systems, which facilitate connections wherever the machinery itself may be located within the factory.

Whatever your choice of sector, it's crucial to gain the appropriate experience with an employer throughout your apprenticeship. There are very few contractors, if any at all, who operate across all of the domestic, commercial and industrial sectors.

CHAPTER 6

THE REGULATIONS

For over 100 years, the UK has been on a journey to continually develop and produce a standard for all electrical installations.

Electrical installations can be incredibly varied, ranging from the average domestic household, which is at its simplest with circuits incorporating lighting and small power rings/radials, to the very large industrial motors with on-site electrical generation. All of these, in some way, must be covered by regulations. This chapter covers some of the primary regulations you'll need to understand as an electrical apprentice.

BS 7671

It's important to remember that the regulations detailed within BS 7671 aren't legislative requirements (required by law), unlike The Electricity at Work Regulations 1989. However, they can be used against you in a court of law if you aren't able to justify why a design or installation doesn't comply with these standards. Then you may well be facing a large fine or even a prison sentence. It's also equally important to remember that diverting from the regulations is acceptable if it's justifiable and safe.

As an overview, the regulations are structured in a way that goes deeper into the specific details the further you read through its pages. It starts out with the fundamental principles and progresses to safety. It then moves on to selecting and erecting equipment, requirements for inspection and testing, and ends with special locations and functional requirements. At nearly 600 pages, it's a mammoth undertaking for anyone – let alone an apprentice – to get to grips with the regulations.

The regulations have been put together by a panel of industry experts known as JPEL/64 (where JPEL stands for Joint Power and Electrical, and the number 64 was handed out by the International Electrotechnical Commission [IEC] – the international body that sets global standards), with this forum comprising engineers representing sectors, specialisms, contractors and leaders within the electrical contracting world. It's facilitated by the Institution of Engineering and Technology (IET), which also publishes the books and accompanying guidance notes that go hand in hand with the regulations book. This includes the *On-Site Guide*.[14] This book is probably the most useful one for you, or any apprentice, to use during your apprenticeship. It breaks down key aspects of installations, giving diagrams and reference tables.

There are many other guidance notes to assist with a deep dive into specific aspects of electrical installations. Many electricians might consider it an unnecessary expense to buy these. However, the information they contain isn't to be underestimated and can in many instances clarify the grey areas (of which there are many) on how to apply the regulations within installations.

In recent years, we've seen the introduction of surge protection devices and arc fault detection devices. Whilst these devices were almost certainly being utilised across many industrial applications, they'd been neglected domestically. Incidents where lives have been lost have refocused the industry on these devices, and they're now included mandatorily in domestic installations.

New terms such as "prosumer" have been coined. Rather than households simply being consumers of electricity, the home generation and injection of electricity into the grid via solar panels, battery storage and EVs mean we're now able to feed power back into the local networks and the National Grid.

In the last few decades, we've also seen developments in the field of RCDs. These have progressed from being separate devices protecting entire installations to the present-day single module devices integrated as residual current breakers with overload protection (RCBOs). You can also explore the type of RCD you'd like to protect your circuit: AC, A, B or F. This has created many nuances within the selection and erection of electrical designs. Understanding these subtle differences is key, and it's well worth developing a good knowledge of these as you and the industry progress.

Many electricians will still be utilising rule-of-thumb principles established during their formative years as an electrical apprentice. However, now is the time to follow the regulations a little more closely and develop with the new technology, which is going to come thick and fast in both the short and long term.

Getting educated on the regulations can be challenging, particularly when this is included in the many years of an already exhaustive apprenticeship. Though it should be noted that most educators will simply be using past papers to educate the trainees to pass the exam, rather than teaching the fundamental principles held within the regulations book.

Again, with it having a relatively low pass mark and being an open-book exam, we can challenge how much value the qualification holds when you don't even have to get two-thirds of it correct. Then again, many still fail the exam, so there's definitely a balance to be had.

The Electricity at Work Regulations 1989

This crucial regulation within the electrical industry is probably the number one document that, whilst enforceable by law, is the *least* understood by those within the electrical industry. There are potentially a few close runners to that statement – for example, the Health and Safety at Work Act 1974 – but after all, this is *the* electrical industry, so you'd think it would be necessary to understand this.

The Electricity at Work Regulations 1989 apply to all aspects of the use of electricity within the workplace. It places a duty on everyone to prevent danger and to facilitate carrying out work on electrical systems in a way that prevents danger.

Whilst, like BS 7671, this encompasses the word "regulations", it's important to understand the difference between statutory and non-statutory regulations (this being the former and BS 7671 being the latter).

Unlike BS 7671, this isn't a large document. First published in 1989 (as its name suggests), it has long been used and rarely modified, with only two subsequent editions amending the original text in almost 40 years (at the time of writing, the last update occurred in 2015).

It's very much written in the form of a legal document and places clear legislative responsibilities on people in their roles within a business. It uses terms such as "duty holder" to ensure clarity. It also isn't just for the persons managing or completing the electrical works as it also covers engineers who may be involved in the design too. We all have a responsibility for guaranteeing electrical safety.

Through various scenarios in industry, one example being during a competent person scheme assessment, it's required that you demonstrate a copy is available and printed, although not necessarily understood (it's worth noting that the Health and Safety Executive [HSE] website offers a free download of this). However, there aren't many scenarios or educational settings where this legislative document is taught, even during apprenticeships.

The document outlines key terms and definitions for the industry, such as "live working" (which includes utilising test equipment!), and it also provides guidance on the interpretation of each regulation and how it would be enforced; for example, "Regulation 29 applies only in criminal proceedings. It provides a defence for a duty holder who can establish that they took all reasonable steps and exercised all due diligence."[15]

> When embarking on this journey of becoming an electrician, it's a must for everyone to understand what ensures compliance with electrical safety, not just for businesses but for every person, regardless of their position.

This is a relatively short section for such an important document relating to the electrical industry, but there's no point paraphrasing it. Instead, if you want to work in the electrical industry, go and pick up a copy and give it a read.

More Regulations

This is the one section that has the greatest risk that it could go on *forever*. To touch on and list every other regulation and/ or standard that an electrician may delve into would be nigh on impossible, let alone to give the detail within the parameters of these pages. Therefore, we'll just touch on the most common ones!

As discussed within the previous sections on regulations, the industry is now beginning to employ new technology, such as surge protection devices, within homes. Over a few revisions, BS 7671 has gradually introduced these into the standard consumer unit arrangement within an installation. However, BS 7671 isn't the standard that should be referred to if you wish to understand surge protection in more detail. For this, you should look at BS EN 62305 (where "BS EN" denotes a British standard harmonised with a European standard).

When you open this standard, you'll notice very quickly that this is the standard for lightning protection. As every apprentice learns, for those buildings large enough to have lightning protection on their external fascias, there's a fundamental requirement to link the electrical systems within the buildings to the lightning protection, which requires the electrical designers and installers to give some thought as to how this is done. Now this doesn't just cover strikes (or strokes) from the sky, it also covers large discharges of electricity in the vicinity of your installation. This is where surge protection comes in! Selecting and installing these devices within consumer units is now within an electrician's scope, hence the overlap of references from within the pages of BS 7671 to the BS EN 62305 standard.

In recent amendments to the regulations, a light (pardon the pun) has been shone on emergency lighting. This needs to be considered with regard to the cabling and electrical infrastructure needed for the escape routes, via hallways and staircases, that are vital to being able to get out of a burning building. If you install lighting within commercial properties – for example, an office or a warehouse – having an emergency lighting system is critical for managing the egress of the many people who will work within that building.

This is where BS 5266 steps in to provide guidance on these installations. This ranges from system design to the varying requirements in different use premises, even detailing the varying illuminance required for rooms in power-failure scenarios. As highlighted earlier, the necessity of this being used during a fire could be key to saving lives, making it imperative to also have a good understanding of BS 5389.

BS 5389 is the regulation for fire detection and fire alarm systems for buildings. There will be angst amongst electricians to define fire engineers separately. It has its own sub-genre of works and specifications. Whilst electricity use can be generalised, it should be clear to anyone who's received the training on either side of this coin that an electrician isn't a fire engineer and a fire engineer isn't an electrician.

If you work on construction sites, you might not just be involved in the build itself but also in the temporary electrics that facilitate the build. For example, throughout this country's construction sites, 110V lighting and small power will be wired up by those following BS 7375 guidance. Again, whilst skills are transferable, having an in-depth knowledge of the risks that come from these ever-evolving sites is key when it comes to designing and implementing them.

If you've ever attended a trade show or large indoor event, you might notice the electrics that power many of the show's stalls and stands. All these will need to have been installed in line with another regulation: BS 7909.

Whilst this list could go on and on, another crucial standard with which to close this chapter is BS EN 60079: explosive atmospheres. We interact with such installations every day – for example, petrol stations – without even realising that's what they are. If you're installing electrical systems within a more industrial setting, then this could include environments where dust and gases occur. All the equipment must be highly sealed and utilise specific earthing arrangements, double pole devices and intrinsically safe voltage-limiting barriers to name but a few.

However, whatever specialism you embark on, there are no limitations on how far you can go.

The Gap

Perhaps the one set of regulations that has garnered the most vitriol within this industry would be Part P of the Building Regulations. Introduced in 2005 for domestic properties, it breaks down installations into two categories: minor and notifiable works.

As its name suggests, "minor works" covers the extension or modification of existing circuits (utilising the minor works installation certificate from the appendices of BS 7671). "Notifiable works" covers installing a new circuit or circuits, consumer unit replacements, or works in a special location as defined by BS 7671.

Part P is aimed at notifying local building control in an endeavour to ensure works are signed off by an electrician registered with a competent person scheme provider. Ultimately, the responsibility will sit with the homeowner or landlord. If a homeowner can't verify that works carried out on their property are in accordance with building regulations, they can face possible criminal charges and be asked to remove said works.

However, Part P has an associated scope gap in that it doesn't capture electrical installation condition reports. There's no legal requirement that deals suitably with this element of work undertaken by electricians. There will be those already registered with competent person schemes who'll naturally, through their own assessments, have their certifications and reports reviewed.

To reduce the regulatory scope gap of Part P, new legislation has been introduced surrounding rental properties, which requires a minimum of five-yearly electrical inspections. This has now fuelled a recent industry bubble. There's been a rush to provide cheap and competitively priced electrical installation condition reports, which has resulted in an influx of inaccurate reports being raised for properties that, if inspected properly, wouldn't be given a satisfactory report.

We'll discuss the race to the bottom in more detail in the next chapter, but this includes companies charging per circuit that are simply providing themselves with insufficient time to complete adequate inspections and all necessary tests.

The other aspect creating a grey area is the interface with other trades, which is something every electrician may be familiar with. There will be those trades that will encroach on the electrical trade.

Plumbers have a common direct interface with electrical installations, in that heating systems are typically the interface point between the two trades. After installing a specific type of heating system for many years, it's understandable that a plumber might become familiar with how to install aspects of the electrical systems associated with it; they may believe that working from an existing switched fused connection unit is within their remit and that the extent of electrical regulations doesn't apply beyond it. Some may even have undergone limited training, such as safe isolation training, as they may need to operate electrical installations safely to complete their own works. Again, the responsibility for certification lies with the homeowner to understand this. So, who, if anyone at all, is explaining this to them?

CHAPTER 7

THE BUSINESS MINDSET

The Dark Art of Quotations and Tenders

Moving from working with the tools and into an office environment can be a challenge for those fortunate enough to undertake this career step to no longer being a "working spark". Beginning a journey into management, if you're fortunate enough to be given this opportunity, is something that not all electricians will get a chance to do.

It does take a very different skill set to work in an office environment compared to the ones that make you a valued electrician. Few make the leap successfully. As an electrician, producing quality installations, having a good understanding of certification and utilising skills during fault-finding are just some of the varied practical skills required to fulfil your role. However, in management, most of the new skills you'll need will be soft ones. Rather than operating a drill, you'll be operating a laptop with design software or using a phone.

There are many things you'll need to learn to be able to step into the role of a project manager. Outside the formal training you can undertake, which might include technical learning such as the City & Guilds 2396 design course, there are skills you can only learn through experience. Predominantly, you'll be learning through the pain of getting it wrong, sometimes financially.

One such aspect of the job is creating quotations and tenders, which many consider to be a dark art. It's a skill no one gets 100% right all the time. With every job, you might win one day and lose the next. It all depends on how much you win by and how much you lose by overall. By winning and losing, I am, of course, referring to profit and loss. Every business aims to at least break even, and most wish make as much as possible as fast as possible.

> Providing quotations is the first step along the way. Whether you're a multimillion-pound business operating in the centre of London or a sole trader operating in Norfolk, providing quotations is a necessity.

So, what's a quotation? It needs to be thought of as more than just a price. That's obviously a fundamental part of it, but it also serves as a contract between you and your customer. It will lay out what you will and won't complete as part of the contracted works. If you aren't working from any plans or drawings, which can happen (typically, at a domestic level), then this will be your only opportunity to state your material allowances clearly. A typical encroachment will be the addition of sockets, as a homeowner works out what they need and how they want to utilise their property. For example, obviously, being able to refer to a statement for the provision of 20 sockets, rather than the 25 now required, enables it to be managed in an open and fair way. This is never a guarantee of work being paid, but it should provide some protection. Ambiguity here will be a financial risk.

Domestically, a quotation can also be an opportunity to set out the terms and conditions for your work (though that may be supplied as a separate document). Here, you can set out whatever you want the terms for payment to be. You can also look to include a variety of clauses to cover scenarios that may occur, such as late payment or how additional works will be managed. However, for commercial and industrial contracts, the terms and conditions (including payment terms) will be client-led.

The fundamental item that everyone looks at, though, is the price. As mentioned previously, being able to price a job well every time is a dark art. It does become more complicated the larger the project is and the greater the number of people that are involved. The time losses that can occur on bigger projects make it more challenging to price accurately yet competitively.

Within the construction industry, it's impossible to perfect the accuracy of your quotes. Accounting for every instance of every material is equally impossible.

Tenders and quotations take time to produce. A client for a particularly large project will want a higher level of accuracy and give you more time to create the quotation, as the risk associated with having omitted scope elements that were unbudgeted for and only identified later can hurt a project, particularly when there's no further capital to support an increased budget.

There are many factors to consider when putting together a price, even down to the person completing the installation work; for example, whether they are fast, slow, capable or even qualified to do the work can sometimes be a factor. You may even decide to reduce your overhead/profit margins depending on how eager you are to win the work.

Each and every factor, if wrongly assessed in advance of the works, provides an element of risk that needs to be managed.

Risk

There are many risks associated with running a project that you'll need to consider as a project manager or business owner, and some of the key ones to be aware of are detailed in this section.

Producing a schedule of materials is a skill in and of itself. Whilst the construction industry is moving into the future with building information modelling (BIM) in the form of three-dimensional (3D) models, most businesses will classically still operate from two-dimensional (2D) drawings. They'll create an informal design so they're able to submit a price, before actually designing the solution once the contract is awarded – at which point, they'll find out how accurate they have or haven't been (as the case may be). There's obviously a considerable risk here that the schedule of materials based on the initial design will not accurately reflect what's actually required for the full design.

As a project manager, safety is the most critical thing you'll have responsibility for. To ensure fundamental compliance with the Health and Safety at Work Act 1974, alongside other regulations such as The Electricity at Work Regulations 1989, you may need to produce risk assessments, create method statements, complete site surveys, understand access equipment, and undergo required training and education. This includes domestically where the major risks are still not fully appreciated, such as the presence of asbestos, which is still a huge concern.

Staff are the backbone of any business. We've already discussed some of the difficulties associated with managing people, and the same applies whether you're standing opposite them with a hard hat on or in the office, wearing a suit and tie. The biggest additional headache and responsibility that comes with running a business at any level can be the problem of increasing or decreasing the number of employed staff. If you don't get your staffing numbers right, it could impact your ability to complete the project on time and also the profit you'll make. It's why using agency labour has become so prevalent in the industry. For a manager, the flexibility to hire and fire without any contractual repercussions is a blessing (this sounds harsh, but it's true).

Whether we're undertaking larger projects, such as a large-scale commercial installation of offices across 10 floors, or doing a small socket outlet replacement in a one-bedroom apartment, time is a factor for us all – particularly if a quotation has been given or a tender price agreed. This can help or hinder the project's bottom line.

For projects with larger values, creating a programme can be a contractual requirement. (If you'd like to learn more, research the New Engineering Contract [NEC] type of contracts commonly used in construction; other contract types are also available.) After all the negotiations, you'll have agreed a price that fits in with the client's budget. However, you can immediately make or break your budget by agreeing on a programme that far exceeds your allowed timeframes.

Most large construction projects will give you an outline at tender in the form of an already developed programme, so the risk may be overexaggerated. However, there's truth in there. If you've submitted a contractual first programme, this is what you must deliver to. If you've priced four guys for eight weeks, but now the client wants you to deliver in six weeks, you'll need to find 25% more labour. Do the guys just work weekends? Longer hours? Or do you hire agency staff to supplement your employed staff? These are considerations for a project manager, who must balance delivery, profit, safety and more when making these decisions. What if it ends up taking eight weeks and you've spent more on labour to achieve the same timeline?

All these decisions come with risk. In the commercial world, risk can mean something different. It isn't a situation that's exposing you to *physical* danger; it's a situation exposing you to *commercial* danger. This could be with respect to either the programme or the budget. This could be the risk of additional scope being added or the likelihood that an engineering problem will occur.

Managing risk is an everyday task for project managers and companies up and down the country.

Profit

Profit: the be all and end all for businesses. Now this isn't a book on how to run an electrical contracting business, but it's important to be able to put yourselves into an employer's shoes when entering the industry. It can make what look like irrational decisions seem very sensible, and vice versa. This is applicable at all levels, whether you're an apprentice in year one or an electrician almost approaching retirement. If you're in a business, it's important to know what that business's goals are.

Many, if not all, will simply want to receive their payslip at the end of the week/month and go home. Many of us will also want to continue to push for an increase in pay, and therein lies a problem for a business.

The priority of a business is to cover its costs first. Everything that's needed to operate a business is a cost. This can range from insurances, staff and memberships to competent person schemes, premises, vehicles, etc. These are all the overheads that are required before a single cable is installed and boots are on-site.

All the costs described as "overheads" kick in before you've even won any work. You'll spend time providing quotations, but you might win only one in four of the jobs you've spent time pricing. Then, if you're lucky enough to win some work, you must factor in the material costs. Businesses will look to add a mark-up on this time and energy spent sourcing products and materials to meet the specific requirements. Depending on how busy the business is, you may decide to inflate this or cut it down to win work. The idea being that, if you're already busy, any more work you take on needs to be even more profitable to compensate for the extra hassle.

This idea of taking on more work and making more profit is a fallacy. Ultimately, you're stretching the resources of your business further, and a customer or two is likely to be upset with your service as a result. It's a balancing act most don't achieve.

In contrast to all of this is the one-man band, who can operate without staff and without premises, amongst many other things. Thus they're able to provide cheaper services with lower overhead costs. Most one-man bands won't hire apprentices. It scary to make the commitment to employ staff, and even more so in the form of non-profitable staff. When applying for jobs, it's worthwhile doing your research and asking the questions.

So, does a company have to make profit? The short answer is no, but by the very definition of profit, if you aren't making a profit, you're making a loss (or walking the tightrope of breaking even). It's very dangerous for a business to aim to break even. Whilst it's a tightrope all businesses walk, aiming for profit is just common sense. Who doesn't like profit?

Profit sharing is something that can also motivate staff. When you've had a good year or even just a reasonable year, sharing profit in the form of bonuses can really be a morale booster for a team. Some might say, "Well, they don't share the losses," and in the end, that's a decision for every business owner.

It's important for every person in the team, no matter how big or small their role is, to understand the needs of the business. Those who don't just might not have a job for much longer...

The Race to the Bottom

The availability of work versus the number of skilled people to complete that work is predominantly what creates a race to the bottom. When there's plenty of work out there, competition will be low, prices can rise and no one struggling to make ends meet – in theory.

The reality is that, as mentioned previously, the electrical industry is undergoing an ever-increasing skills shortage. Fewer people are entering the industry and completing apprenticeships. Businesses are using cheaper labour to supplement their workforces and complete the more rudimentary tasks of electrical installation, such as installing containment (tray, trunking, etc.), and then bringing in the experienced, qualified electrician to inspect and test upon completion – saving thousands along the way.

This influx of cheaper labour from various routes of entry into the electrical industry – and in particular, the domestic market, which can sit largely unregulated, unmonitored and untethered – has created what's commonly known as "the race to the bottom". This means everyone competing, undercutting and under-pricing in order to win contracts and work – and to put some food on the table.

However, there's a growing anti-culture within the industry: those who'll walk away from work and commit to not under-price, reduce margins or quality to win work. They'll argue they're providing a sustainable income for the long-term success of their business – not just in terms of financial power but also in reputation.

Let's look at an example, albeit an extreme example.

It has been known within the industry for electrical installation condition reports to be undertaken for £5–10 a circuit. Typically, a domestic property will have somewhere in the region of five to ten circuits. For example, lights up and down, sockets up and down, cooker circuit, boiler and now you'll likely see EV charging point circuits also – totalling seven circuits. This creates total earnings for this example inspection of £70.

What's not understood by clients (homeowners in this instance), who just want that bit of paper detailing a clean bill of health for their property, is the amount of work that can go into an electrical installation condition report.

A diligent electrician will remove all sockets, light fittings and power points; verify the wiring in the loft and potentially even under floorboards (I can hear the groans of electricians reading this); review distribution equipment; inspect incoming water and gas; and have a good working knowledge of the regulations in BS 7671 from which to derive a level of compliance in their minds after many years of training. All these activities and more take time. Time costs money. Therefore, the price will reflect the amount of time needed. It should be straightforward.

If the average electrician is charging £35 per hour (even bigger groans), that gives you two hours to inspect the property if you're to compete with the offer of £70. For the average three-bedroom house these days, the diversity of equipment, circuits and electronics installed and available is going to require those inspecting households to have more knowledge, combined with experience, and both acquired over many years.

The person completing the "drive-by" inspection and test might race around getting test values, with no consideration for many varying factors. They might simply test the RCD (assuming one is present) and say that's good enough to ensure safety for peace of mind.

But what if there were an EV charging point with both an earth rod and an O-PEN device installed, fostering a myriad of different earthing issues? This simply wouldn't be covered, and the homeowner would be no better informed than they were before the inspection. Except, this time, they've got a piece of paper to disillusion them into believing they're compliant and safe.

They need to try not to worry about the limitations highlighted in the report, such as a "10% visual inspection of *external* items only". For those reading this who may not understand that kind of statement, it means the inspector has potentially only looked at one in ten sockets present in the household and possibly without even removing it/them.

Ultimately, this responsibility to not be drawn into a race to the bottom might be unavoidable, depending on your local competition, but it's down to those who run the businesses holding this responsibility to work together to not let it define them.

Agency Work

For many years now, there has been an internal struggle within the electrical industry between those who are employed and those who are self-employed. You may hear those who are self-employed being referred to as "agency workers" on some construction sites. Predominantly, this means they're guns for hire.

There are many pros and cons to utilising agency workers and, similarly, to working as a self-employed electrician or even apprentice!

Typically, you'll see this type of labour used on larger projects, but this doesn't mean smaller projects don't make use of agency labour. Self-employed electricians who work on a short-term basis for projects don't come cheap. These are workers who don't receive any of the benefits of employment – such as holiday, sick pay, vehicles, fuel, etc. – so all this cost is factored into the overheads of their working day.

There has long been a perception that these rates are overinflated. A variety of things feed into this: the skills gap, the type of installation work required (for example, someone who's familiar with the type of installation work you want undertaken), industry rates, availability, qualifications and more.

There are risks to loading up your labour force with agency labour. They might want to leave and will be able to do so with zero notice. They might leave for a variety of reasons, including pay (yes, you might be outbid). It might be difficult to even find the right personnel to build a team for a project. In the end, you'll take the best engineers you can find. However, paying a high price for someone who isn't as competent as you'd like can be a painful experience.

Agency workers might struggle to be motivated. They might not be invested in the project being profitable or the company succeeding. In the long run, the only one who keeps the employer's interests at heart is themself.

However, there are always exceptions to the rule, and many agency workers within the industry don't operate on these principles. They can be relied upon and are very much seen as being worth every penny. In the same way as homeowners find a reliable tradesperson and stick with them, a contractor will always go back to the same good people once they've discovered them. They might even try to employ them!

The pros of being employed are the reverse of the cons of being self-employed. Some of those employed staff working alongside agency workers might feel resentment at the inflated rates of those working alongside them who have much less responsibility. Ultimately, they have the security of an employer who'll find them work and endeavour to keep them employed whilst honouring an employment contract.

One benefit of being an agency worker is being your own boss; for example, you don't have to take an opportunity or job that you don't want to do. Assuming qualifications aren't an issue, this can be a major stumbling block for those who work in this manner, and it inhibits the maximum they can earn in a day.

Agency workers can have their pay structured in different ways. You might look at hourly rates so you can watch every penny. Alternatively, you can pay a day rate and try to maximise their output. Whether you employ staff or use self-employed staff, you need to motivate your team!

Directors and Shareholders

There's a further level to managing a business, and it's entered once you've passed the threshold to become a director or shareholder. To some, this can be the most daunting thing that they'll undertake. Registering with Companies' House, listing the business as a limited company and having shares, and if you're working within a larger company, there's also the challenge of having a board of directors and shareholders.

Once that leap has been made, one of the major differences is the legal responsibilities now placed on your head. These go hand in hand with the moral responsibilities we all hold, but not everyone has the strictest of morals...

The law sets out what's called "the general duties of a director".[16] There's no escaping these rules – no denial and no excuses. This is true even if you're not active in your role of director, you act as a director but haven't been formally appointed, or you control a board of directors without being on it.

The responsibility can weigh heavily if you let it. However, most people never need worry about this. As mentioned earlier, most of us have a conscience that guides us through these turbulent waters.

As a director, you might lay out the company's constitution. These are the written rules about the running of the company, other directors and the company secretary. The constitution sets out what powers you have as a director and the purpose of those powers.

You'll be acting in the company's interests, not necessarily just your own. This is particularly true when it comes to the interests of your employees. Every decision you take can have a profound impact on those around you, in both the short and long term.

One of the hardest pills to swallow is a company becoming insolvent. During a liquidation, it can be tough moving your responsibility from employee to creditor. Businesses fail all the time, but if you can demonstrate to any liquidator that you've acted responsibly, you can start a new business. And therein lies the problem: plenty will seek to abuse the system, and a previous business failure does not deter them.

The second step for any business is having shareholders, and this role is initially likely to be filled by the people who are also acting as directors. Typically, these shareholders are the good folk who invest capital in the business when it needs it. They're also the ones who take the money home when the sun has shone and hay has been made. They have less responsibility, as this predominantly sits with the directors. But nonetheless, they're the oil that can grease the metaphorical wheels of a business.

When acting as a limited company, as mentioned previously, it will typically be the same person who's judge, jury and executioner. The electrical industry is filled with small to medium-sized enterprises (SMEs). For those who earn enough to warrant moving to become a limited company, there are many benefits, such as the manipulation of value added tax (VAT).

Many will prefer to continue under the sole-trader umbrella and avoid all these legal ramifications. Whoever you are, having a good accountant is always imperative to helping you make the decision on whether to become a director or a shareholder – or not.

Programme

When working in construction, one thing above all others will be the focal point in a contract, and that's the programme. The construction industry has a notorious reputation for going over budget and over time. There are a million factors that contribute to why a programme may or may not be achieved, from minor changes made by a client during construction to the monumental disaster of missed detail in the design.

The programme will be the opportunity to get all trades together in one place to align all the project goals and work out the best fit, timing and placement of the works each trade must achieve. When done unrealistically on a domestic project, this could result in an error as simple as planning for the plasterers to commence their works prior to the electricians, who then chase every wall and make a mess of everything – literally!

Let's get real, though; domestically, you're unlikely to see a formal programme of works. Instead, it will be a loose framework that everyone who's worked in the domestic sector will understand. The sequencing is tried and tested, and it's only communicated verbally, if at all.

The larger projects and construction companies will take a different stance on having a programme. When you have millions of pounds at risk, including contractual penalties in the form of liquidated damages, you're more likely to take it seriously. Liquidated damages are when a contractor sets milestones that must be achieved within a contract. This can be completing construction by a certain date and/or any milestone in between that's agreed mutually as part of the contract. Miss that key date and your company will be open to liquidated damages – sometimes in the form of a daily penalty until the works are completed.

One way larger construction companies will oversee the process is by hiring a planner. This is someone whose job is to manage the programme and highlight delays as early as possible (amongst other things).

Planning, much like quoting, has its own skill set. Being able to look at a task, understand how long it will take and predict this with accuracy isn't something many achieve within the electrical industry, let alone in the construction industry. Drawing up a programme as part of a tender submission can very clearly outline how you've worked out the costs you have. Including such a programme, which is typically done in contracts, means it's easier to track delays, what you planned to do, where it has gone wrong and, most importantly, who's to blame. Someone (yes, there's *always* someone) will have to pick up the bill, and this might be your business if the programme isn't managed properly.

It's always good to consult the construction team at the commencement of any project, even if timelines and expectations are communicated only verbally. Telling someone a job must be completed in five days with no resources to do so won't end well.

It's common on projects that, once the crap hits the metaphorical fan, the programme goes out the window. This is probably the worst time to do that. However, unless there's a project manager, no subcontractor will want to take total ownership. The customer isn't the best person to do this either (you only need watch an episode or two of *Grand Designs* to discover this).

Ensuring there are realistic expectations all round is the key to any programme. The only thing then is maintaining it.

CHAPTER 8

THE ONLY CERTAINTIES IN LIFE ARE DEATH AND TAXES

Limited Companies

Operating as a sole trader can be a very tough life. When working as a sole trader, the slim line between your business bank account and your personal bank account can become non-existent – in many cases they're one and the same thing. It can also provide its own challenges in terms of employment and the administering of so many aspects of a business.

This is why many, even when operating as a single-person enterprise, will opt to register as a limited company. It can draw a line in the sand between you and your business.

Acting as a sole trader and facing the risk that, if trading becomes difficult, it can impact your personal savings or even the roof over your head (if you're lucky enough to be a home owner) can be too much for some to risk. Becoming a limited company does exactly what it says on the tin: it limits the business's finances to the business itself and not to you.

One of the perks of setting up a limited company comes from navigating the choppy seas of VAT. This can be added to anything and everything. The benefit of operating as a limited company is that you can charge VAT on your services as an electrician, which can be offset against VAT you spend.

There's also a variety of schemes that assist businesses in this regard, one of which is the VAT Flat Rate Scheme. The scheme is based on business performance and turnover; you can explore charging the required 20%, but then only paying a much lower percentage based on the type of business you run, and as mentioned already, its financial performance. It's always worth being aware that there's lots of support out there to help a business or a person in their hour of need.

Working as a limited company can also give you flexibility with how you manage the finances of your business. That includes taking out business loans – again, so they aren't tied to you individually. In the fantastic situation of being in profit, you can also decide to reinvest in the business, and the money doesn't have to leave your personal bank account to do so. The tougher decisions come when the business isn't making a profit.

A business may require further investment from its owners, whether it's a new start-up or a struggling established business. Owning a business doesn't mean you're immune from losing money. Most will care about their business in a way that's akin to a parent's relationship with one of their children. They want to see it succeed and stand on its own two feet before they run off into the sunset.

However, the truth is that most businesses fail before reaching their third birthday.[17]

One way or another, you'll end up paying the government the tax it's owed for the business and as an employee. Whether you're paying yourself a salary or not, you'll pay National Insurance and income tax. If you've ever taken out a student loan, you'll also see that as a nice big deduction. Then there are pensions. With an ever-increasing cost of living, pensions are a lifeline for many. The government may match pension contributions, encouraging employers to put something away for the future; however, should you withdraw it, it will be taxed.

If you say, "I don't want to take a big salary; I've got no guaranteed income," then the alternatives include looking at how you can pay yourself as and when needed. This will typically be completed through dividends. You'll be paying yourself what your business can afford and paying the rest almost on an ad hoc basis in the form of dividends. Now if you think you're escaping paying tax by going via this route, you'd be wrong.

A salary is a business expense. An overhead. A cost. Something your business knows it must pay before it can review profit or losses. If you artificially keep your salary low, then when your business ultimately does earn money, that's going to be considered profit. That's when corporation tax will kick in. You'll then look to pay yourself a dividend. That's when dividend tax will walk through the next door. There are also bands for these taxes in the same way as there are for income tax; the more you earn, the more you're liable to be taxed for.

There's a distinct difference between tax avoidance and evasion. Both are negative, and ensuring an accountant is in place to help you clearly understand how best to manage the finances of your business is as critical as anything else you can do when establishing a business.

Times are moving fast in the 21st century, with the rise of electronics not just within the electrical industry but also within the financial world. The world is becoming a cashless society. In recent years since the Covid-19 pandemic, we've gone from most people carrying cash to putting our card into machines and entering PINs, tapping contactless cards with ever-increasing limits, or where there's now no physical card but it's represented in the electronic wallet on your mobile phone.

The domestic market will need to develop rapidly to keep up with this trend. More businesses will need to expect immediate payment via internet-linked card payment devices. The days of invoicing for domestic work and then waiting for a period before being paid is changing quickly. More and more electricians are reducing risk by making certain up-front deposits are taken to secure work, which reassures them and their businesses that they'll be able to pay all the bills.

In this modern world, there's a decrease in the number of customers wanting to avoid paying the VAT on a bill by paying in cash, and the traceability of transactions is key. Performing electronic transfers has made accounting much easier to do, for both accountants and business owners. No longer are they having to thumb through invoices, receipts and paperwork. It's all managed electronically, linked to an accounting system and uploaded automatically. Time will decide if that's ultimately a good thing or not.

Either way, long gone are the days of sifting through receipts, bills and unaccounted for bits of paper.

Inside or Outside?

It was Benjamin Franklin, a founding father of the United States of America, who coined the phrase "In this world, nothing is certain except death and taxes." This certainly is a truth that has stood the test of time since those words were initially spoken. No words spoken are truer for electricians than these.

There's a perception from yesteryear that all tradespeople are avoiding taxes in some manner or another, ripping their customers or the government off. The suggestion of working for cash to avoid various taxes is one that's fading with an increasingly electronically driven financial system. Customers are now very protected through traceable electronic transactions.

There may be many of us who avoid such issues and enter the world of employment, never gazing at our payslips' other columns that detail all the lovely subtractions heading off to be managed through local and national government budgets.

This isn't the place to get into the basics of society and the fundamental principles on which to build one. However, in the 21st century, there's a growing minority that feels frustration at a construction industry that's progressively more financially regulated.

One such instance is the introduction and subsequent rulings surrounding the infamous IR35. As a very brief summary, this legislation was brought in around 1999. Designed as an anti-avoidance tax legislation, it was intended to ensure that those who were utilising loopholes in the law to manipulate the amount of tax they paid were caught in the metaphorical government net. It effectively surrounds the status of single personnel working as limited businesses.

There are limits to earnings where, once you cross a particular financial threshold, it becomes more necessary to make the change from operating as a sole trader to a limited company. There are hundreds of clarifications surrounding IR35, and we certainly won't be exploring those within the pages of this book. However, it essentially boils down to how someone, when acting as a business, interacts with other businesses. If you deem yourself to be a limited company and then undertake a form of work where you're providing your services to another business, whilst not doing so for any other businesses, you're in effect "employed" by the company that's requested your services. Therefore, by registering as a limited company, you might be avoiding paying taxes an employee might pay if they were to be a permanent employee of said business, such as National Insurance, income tax, etc.

There are so many caveats to this scenario as to make every situation unique. These are made via assessments on government websites. Assuming this is acceptable, this would then clarify you as working outside IR35.

In 2021, the emphasis of the law was refocused; instead of the individual having the responsibility to ensure their taxes were being handled compliantly, the businesses that "employed" those individuals became the liable ones if they weren't properly administering the taxes.

This ruling forced many of those operating as limited companies to move from outside IR35 to be inside IR35. This meant that the typical employment taxes as mentioned earlier would need to be paid. This is commonly completed by the person in question being hired through an agency – what's termed an "umbrella company". These effectively pay the taxes of an employed person, without any of the benefits such as sick pay or holiday pay, though they may retain pay to provide some facilities such as the perception of holiday pay. The majority will opt for a cash-now approach and manage their own finances in house. There's no right or wrong way to approach this.

Rates of pay are often much higher for those operating on shorter-term contracts, which is why the construction industry – not just the electrical industry – has so many people who work in this way. They're able to maintain a higher income (albeit without the benefits).

The impact of this was that it simply drove many into taking up permanent employment or finding those who still operate outside of IR35. Many industries have taken a zero-tolerance policy of hiring inside IR35 agencies only, thus removing all grey areas when considering taxes and guaranteeing responsibility throughout their supply chain.

This can cause division on sites and projects, with many of those who are employees feeling short-changed when working alongside their higher-paid agency counterparts. The balancing act of employment versus agency work is one that will drag on forever. The key thing is for you to do what's right for you. Agency working comes with risk: there's a lack of financial support but higher pay to cover those times of uncertainty.

The important thing is to always employ a suitably qualified and experienced accountant who can assist you and verify where you stand legally with various taxes and financial arrangements.

CHAPTER 9

COMPETENT PERSON SCHEMES

The Misconception

There's an incredibly large number of misconceptions about what you can and can't do as an electrician. These will be predominantly held by the public, but some are within the industry itself.

The biggest misconception is how the industry is regulated and who regulates it, with the belief being that a competent person scheme regulates everyone and everything operating within said industry. Unfortunately, this simply isn't true – although most within the industry wish it were!

There are several competent person schemes operating within the electrical industry. The two most prominent ones currently are the NICEIC and NAPIT, as mentioned earlier. The former is the most widely recognised by those outside the industry. This is primarily due to it being created in 1923 and incorporated in 1956. It has long been synonymous with the electrical industry. The latter was founded as an alternative later in the 20th century to somewhat avoid a monopolistic system.

The key part of the misconception comes from the fact that competent person schemes are a voluntary membership enterprise. Electrical contractors will join via a membership. The membership includes an annual inspection of selected installations, alongside technical reviews of documentation and members of staff who are listed as qualified supervisors. This membership will facilitate more than just these basic items, but these are the major aspects that a member of the public most likely thinks are non-negotiable for every contractor within the industry.

However, there's no legal requirement for any electrical contractor or electrician to register with a competent person scheme. In the same way as others operating in the construction industry will liaise with the local borough via their building control department, this can also be done for the electrical industry. Building control may request mid-installation visits alongside reviews of certification. The main sticking point in this process for most customers (as they're the ones who pay the bills) are the fees associated with going down this avenue. It's worth noting that most local authorities are underfunded whilst charging high fees.

The fees relative to the membership cost of a competent person scheme would be covered by just a handful of applications to the local authority. Thus, this makes the cost-saving benefit an easy and obvious choice for every contractor to pass on to their clients, increasing the likelihood of winning work. It's now widely accepted as the norm within the industry to be registered with a competent person scheme.

These schemes do offer lots of benefits, even if you aren't a member. By following them on various social media platforms, you'll get access to plenty of CPD to get you thinking. If used well, businesses gain lots of advantages from being affiliated with a competent person scheme. Simply bearing the logo on your website / marketing materials can have a substantial influence on the public who hold this misconception.

Several parts of how competent person schemes operate have, in recent years, begun to draw attention – and for some parts this is in the form of criticism.

As mentioned previously, if you were to look at obtaining all the necessary compliance certifications via the local authority, they'd look to complete a minimum of one inspection of the installations, but potentially several at different stages of the project. The way this is managed – or you could say "mitigated" – through a competent person scheme is to complete an annual inspection. At this time, the electrical contractor would offer several installations for an inspector to visit, at which they would walk through and demonstrate both compliance and knowledge in relation to the regulations.

This system, like any other, is open to manipulation. Obviously, the installations to be inspected must be coordinated in advance with the clients. The clients might be unavailable, which therefore makes 99% of the installations unavailable to the inspector. The other side of the coin is that the contractor will likely only make the best installations available (and why wouldn't you?), but is that the purpose?

There's a feeling within the industry that there has been a general decline in standards for some years. Substandard and non-compliant installations are occurring more frequently. Who else, if not the competent person schemes, is meant to deal with such an issue?

As mentioned earlier, whilst it isn't mandated that everyone must be affiliated with a competent person scheme, those who do opt to join will become a member. As a member, you'll have access to lots of benefits that are for members only. These include the latest advice, updates associated with the regulations, and guidance and support from technical staff. As also discussed previously, another advantage is the cost of certification and installation registration being diminished.

One important thing to remember with any type of membership is that, ultimately, without members, what use is the competent person scheme?

Qualified Supervisors

Part of the process when managing installations under the structure of a competent person scheme is the role of a qualified supervisor, who'll be responsible for ensuring quality and compliance. They will replace the local authority inspector as part of that process under the schemes.

Many consider becoming a qualified supervisor to be a stepping stone towards a management position.

The roles and responsibilities of a qualified supervisor typically include reviewing and auditing electrical installations, certification, technical support, and monitoring and managing compliance; a classic example of this is test-equipment calibration.

A company will employ someone within the business to fill this role (unless none are suitably qualified, of course). There are minimum qualifications required to achieve the role of a qualified supervisor. These include the aforementioned NVQ and the inspection and testing qualification, amongst others. There's a further requirement to have been working in the installation scope of the business for at least two years. It's important to note that there are many routes to and qualifications for becoming a qualified electrician. It's imperative to check with the competent person schemes as to what is needed, as things move and change fast!

A fallacy associated with this role is that you may naturally conclude every installation or project a company completes will require its own dedicated qualified supervisor to oversee the quality and compliance of installations, from the first and second fixes to the testing and commissioning. This misconception is often held by those within the electrical industry as well as those outside it. The exact roles of the qualified supervisors within a business will be decided by the company and its management structure.

If the business is a sole trader, there's a limit to the number of people who can operate in said business within the qualified supervisor role.

The role becomes a little more complicated and strained once we begin to scale. If you add 30 employees to an SME, how should you arrange your qualified supervisors? Having one per project might mean you need 15 qualified supervisors. Having one project manager for the business will also mean one qualified supervisor. What about having a ratio of five employees to one supervisor? There are no strict rules for this number of supervisors.

Now scale it up to a large national business with hundreds, if not thousands, of employees: what will the company policy be?

CHAPTER 10

OTHER MEMBERSHIPS

Trade Associations

A trade association is an organisation funded by businesses that operate within a specific industry. Associations may offer other services, such as educational content and specialist resources, including legal advice. Many associations are non-profit organisations governed by bylaws and directed by officers who are also members.

The leading trade association in the electrical industry is the ECA. There are others, but this is the primary one you'll see, and it has the biggest representation in the electrical sector due to its historical significance.

Founded early in the 20th century, the ECA operates as a membership organisation. It ensures its members are kept informed and updated on the latest regulations, and it holds regional meetings where members can discuss the industry and issues of importance to their operation, amongst other things. Many companies working in the industry will likely now be members, although not all.

In addition to membership providing the aforementioned benefits, it also offers legal advice and even contract reviews for those not familiar or seeking assistance with lengthier contracts. Members can also request help with health and safety issues. Whilst most companies working within the commercial and, certainly, the industrial sectors are familiar with risk assessments and method statements, this can be a new challenge for those operating within the domestic sector, where businesses are less conscious of their responsibilities under the eyes of the law to their employees, others and even themselves. Having an expert on the end of a phone to support a business can definitely be useful.

Not every business will see the value in these memberships and will instead view the overhead as an unnecessary cost. Ultimately, if your business won't see the benefit and utilise the membership fully, then this may be true.

The ECA also works with regulatory bodies such as the IET, and ECA technical advisors and members act as representatives on regulatory committees such as JPEL/64. This has created a wide sphere of influence in a sector that's relatively confined to several businesses.

It's worth noting that, as one of the founding institutions present during the initial introduction of electricity into the domestic setting, it's developed along with the industry itself. There are many familiar names that are part of the ECA group, such as Certsure (the parent company of the NICEIC), the JIB and JTL, the latter of which was formed as a training provider in partnership with Unite (the union). In some form, the ECA reaches all aspects of the industry.

The structure of the ECA itself is one based on the regions of the UK. Each ECA region is made up of the active members in the corresponding area of the country, and these then feed into the national structure.

Fees can and do vary for different-sized members to meet their membership requirements.

Joint Industry Board (JIB)

The JIB is an organisation that looks to set the standards for employment and grades of electricians, amongst other activities. It's membership based; however, this membership isn't to be confused with an electrician holding the JIB ECS gold card, which doesn't require membership.

One of the JIB's bigger inputs into the electrical industry is determining the wages for its members. This provides a two-to-three-year forecast that allows JIB members to establish what they should be paying their employees. It details all the various potential scenarios (although I'm sure a few won't necessarily be captured). This can range from being an apprentice to being an approved electrician, and it also depends on whether you provide your own transport or not. The rates are adjusted according to each situation and even location.

There have been lots of discussions within the industry in recent years regarding these determinations. There are some common misconceptions regarding who should be using the pay rates issued by the JIB. It's commonly referenced by contractors who are *not* members of the JIB. Likewise, if an employee refers to those rates in order to get a pay rise, but the company isn't a member, then there's very little chance of enforcing this.

However, if your company *is* a JIB member, there certainly might be avenues to assist with disputing pay rates via the JIB. It would be a risky strategy to negotiate terms with your employer in this manner, though.

The other aspect is the infamous JIB ECS gold card. If you wish to access a construction site in the UK, it's highly likely you'll need to undertake a safety exam as part of the ECS. The process doesn't just include a site safety exam, noting that it differs from the standard CSCS exam by including some electrical-based questions.

Assuming you pass the exam (and not everyone does), you'll then send your qualifications to the JIB, and once verified, an ECS gold card is issued. This card will be clearly dated and include your photo for ID purposes. The qualifications you've achieved will be detailed on the back of the card; more importantly, on the front of the card is your grading. Most apprentices will remember the day they got their ECS gold card with "Electrician" on the front. It's an achievement, but also not the end of the journey!

There's a grading system associated with the grading level that's given on the front of your ECS gold card, based on the qualifications you hold. As discussed in *Chapters 1* and *3*, the sheer range of qualifications and certification bodies makes this a challenge. However, the JIB does have good resources to indicate clearly what grading you should receive. This can range from being a labourer with no electrical qualifications to being an approved electrician holding all relevant qualifications, including the inspection and testing qualification in any of its many historical formats.

The grading system does present issues when considering the older generations of electricians, where qualifications varied or simply didn't exist. With qualifications such as the NVQ level three only coming into existence in the latter part of these electricians' careers, they're unable to evidence their training in the same way as more recently qualified apprentices can.

It's estimated that up to 60,000 industry skills cards were issued under the Industry Accreditation (also known as Grandfather Rights) and can't be renewed. Whilst there has been a sufficient notice period to achieve the required updated qualifications, there will be many who won't complete them in time, whether that's a cost or simply an issue of principle. Many object to the moving target of qualifications.

It has also been suggested that the industry is moving towards being segregated in its qualifications, and there's no longer a one-size-fits-all "electrician" qualification. There's some evidence to support this. However, if you want to work across various sectors in the industry, maintaining qualifications across all fields is critical, and whilst updating your JIB ECS gold card every three years may seem laborious, many view it as money well spent – particularly those in the commercial and industrial sectors.

Money that would *not* be well spent includes any outlay on one of the recent influx of fake ECS gold cards into the construction industry. Throughout the annals of the internet, there have been copious amounts of individuals ready to take your hard-earned money and provide you with a fake card and/or qualification. This has grown to prominence in recent years; as social media has developed further content and accounts for electricians, a new opportunity for criminals has arisen. It's important to remember that these are scams. If you were to fake competency to gain access to a construction site and an accident did occur, what would you tell the judge?

Institution of Engineering and Technology (IET)

Founded in 1871, the IET has a rich history of nurturing innovation and connecting brilliant minds in the field of engineering. Its roots can be traced back to the vision of a few forward-thinking individuals who recognised the need for an organisation that would unite engineers and promote excellence in their work. It has hosted significant historical figures from the world of electricity, such as Nikola Tesla and Michael Faraday, with the latter now commemorated outside the building.

One of the hallmarks of the IET is its commitment to knowledge sharing. Engineers, whether they're seasoned professionals or aspiring students, find a wealth of resources and opportunities within the organisation. The IET's vast library, both physical and digital, houses a treasure trove of engineering literature, from classic texts to cutting-edge research papers. Engineers can access this wealth of knowledge to inform their work and stay abreast of the latest developments in their field, many of which are now accessible through online portals.

The IET's commitment to professional development is another cornerstone of its mission. Through partnerships with universities and institutions worldwide, the IET offers accredited courses and certifications that help engineers enhance their skills and advance their careers. Its comprehensive approach to learning includes online courses, workshops and conferences, which enable engineers to engage with their peers and learn from experts in various domains.

In the modern era of rapid technological advancement, the IET has recognised the importance of fostering innovation. To this end, it provides platforms for engineers and technologists to showcase their groundbreaking work. The IET Innovation Awards celebrate the brightest minds in the industry, highlighting innovations that have the potential to change the world. The winners of these awards are lauded for their dedication to solving real-world problems.

The organisation actively promotes diversity in science, technology, engineering and mathematics (STEM) fields, and it's striving to break down barriers and ensure everyone has an equal opportunity to excel in engineering and technology.

As with professional registration, membership of the IET can be very beneficial for the electrician who wishes to push themself. It has reasonably priced membership options for apprentices, giving access to all of the aforementioned benefits. However, many electricians won't be a member or professionally registered with the IET, but this shouldn't deter you, should you choose to join.

As mentioned earlier, the IET also produces and publishes the electrical regulations under BS 7671. Through various committees, it seeks to review, update and progress the regulations in line with industry developments. One sore point for the industry in recent years has been the cost of the regs book. It's one of the more costly purchases an electrician will make outside of tools. Issues arise, with corrigenda (documented corrections of errors that were inadvertently introduced into the text[18]), amendments and new editions being published every few years. It's expensive to stay current. However, it's important to think of it as an investment in yourself, particularly in the formative years of your of career.

Trade Unions

The purpose of a trade union is to represent and advocate for the interests and rights of its members, who typically share a common occupation, industry or profession. The predominant trade union in the UK's construction industry is Unite.

One of the primary functions of a trade union is to negotiate with employers on behalf of its members to secure better wages, benefits, working conditions and job security. Through collective bargaining, unions aim to achieve favourable employment terms, which might be challenging for individual workers to negotiate on their own.

Trade unions work to ensure that the rights of their members are upheld. They advocate for fair treatment, protection from workplace discrimination, and adherence to labour laws and regulations. In cases of unfair dismissal or unjust treatment, unions often provide legal support to their members.

Unions can also facilitate collective action amongst workers, such as strikes or protests, when negotiations with employers break down or when workers believe their rights or interests are being violated. These actions can put pressure on employers to address workers' concerns. They may also engage in broader social and economic advocacy beyond the workplace, such as participating in political activities, lobbying for labour-friendly policies, and supporting legislation that benefits workers' rights and economic well-being.

Unite holds a distinct position within the electrical industry. It stands as the sole officially acknowledged entity representing operatives employed under the provisions of the JIB Agreement. This recognition encompasses negotiations with the ECA and the representation of members via the JIB disputes procedure. Moreover, exclusive voting rights on wage agreements negotiated under the JIB are given solely to Unite members.

There are many cons to working within a union as well. You might find this increases workplace tension. You have less autonomy to make your own decisions as these could affect others. You may even have to strike without pay, relying on the union to maintain your wages.

Whilst membership of a union comes with the cost of membership fees, if you want to ensure you have some form of support and representation in the workplace, working in groups facilitated by unions might be the best option for you, but it's always best to weigh up all your options first.

CHAPTER 11

CONTINUOUS PROFESSIONAL DEVELOPMENT

What's Continuous Professional Development (CPD)?

CPD is a phrase that's new to the industry. To many, these words trigger a vitriolic response. However, it's something that electricians have always done and will continue to do.

Electricians have never recorded their CPD very well. Displaying your knowledge when it's not been formally presented within a qualification used to be tricky. Now, most within the industry recognise that lots of learning takes place outside a classroom setting. In fact, most of it does. The key is the reflection and subsequent application.

Reflecting on something you've learned is an important step in recognising you've learned and developed your understanding. Application is then a case of implementing the knowledge you've gained. This could be utilising it as part of a design or installation, or simply imparting it to your colleagues.

There are so many ways to source content now, ignoring the qualifications we all undertake (which are more than obvious), including reading manufacturer's instructions on how to install or maintain a product. Even contacting the manufacturer directly for further information can be valuable CPD.

There are so many events up and down the country these days, with trade shows not only exhibiting the latest products and tools. Hosted and presented by the IET and competent person schemes, they also provide lectures and bite-sized seminars on a variety of subjects, including updates to the regulations (which are coming thick and fast with the rapid growth in technology). Don't forget the likes of trade magazines – some of which are now even focusing on providing CPD as part of their monthly editions!

A controversial one might be the online content and social media spaces. Debating online or viewing someone's YouTube content can be just as incredibly useful as sitting in any class. As stated previously, it's about the reflection and application. However, it's vital not to fall into the trap of viewing others' opinions as CPD. Always undertake your own research and gain the information first-hand for your own reflection.

The IET – via its online portal, aptly titled "Career Manager" – now facilitates recording CPD. It has also made it a mandatory requirement to undertake a certain number of hours CPD per year when you're professionally registered. This threshold is low, so most will achieve this easily, and it certainly doesn't put any pressure on those who are busy, so they can keep it ticking over. This is an asset when considering membership of the IET.

Professional Registration

You may have seen people around with lots of initials after their name. Well, this is likely to be one of two things: professional registration to recognise your work or a membership.

For nearly 200 years, the status of becoming a chartered engineer has long been revered; backed by a royal charter, it recognises those who are working at a high level, thus establishing what it means to be an engineer.

The IET dates back almost 150 years – including, in its time, mergers and rebranding (to use modern terminology).

Typically, this is the organisation that will facilitate an electrician's professional registration assessment on behalf of the engineering council – although others are available such as the Chartered Institute of Building Service Engineers (CIBSE).

Five key aspects of competency are assessed for every level of professional registration:

- Knowledge and understanding
- Design, development and solving engineering problems
- Responsibility, management and leadership
- Communication and interpersonal skills
- Personal and professional commitment

These vary depending on the level of registration being applied for.

It's hugely beneficial for any apprentice entering into the electrical industry to review these criteria early into their journey. Should you do this, it could provide direction, inspiration and a clear indication of how to develop yourself throughout your career journey. The IET has many facilities for this, including online portals such as Career Manager, not to mention its online forums.

Predominantly, when assessing themselves at a relevant level, the average electrician should be competent enough to achieve the standards required within an engineering technician (EngTech) application. There are three questions that give you the opportunity to provide examples and details of your underpinning knowledge and understanding. This is alongside providing other information, such as your career history.

The level above this is the incorporated engineer (IEng) status. This will be slightly more difficult to achieve for the average working electrician, but it is doable. Typically, it focuses on design-related activities, including the implementation of scientific principles, alongside the latest industry developments.

As detailed earlier, the highest level of recognition within professional registration is becoming a chartered engineer (CEng).

These statuses are all achieved through a variety of institutions that facilitate the assessment based on the relevant sector.

Becoming a member of an organisation such as the IET can be beneficial for progressing your career. In this case, you would become a MIET (with the M standing for "member") or a TMIET (a "technician member"). Whilst this type of membership doesn't hold the same weight throughout industry as professional registration might, it does show a willingness to better yourself by using the available resources to develop and move forwards, potentially with the goal of becoming professionally registered one day.

There are levels to membership. For those who demonstrate abilities above and beyond the industry norms – in any categories such as responsibility, innovation, enterprise, influence and many others – it offers the opportunity to be assessed again and awarded FIET (a "fellow" of the organisation). This is slightly harder to attain than the standard membership and is appraised by existing fellows against specific criteria.

Ultimately, there are more people in the electrical industry who don't hold any type of membership other than the ones required to complete their days' work more easily. Many will consider these other memberships superfluous, being above and beyond what's required as a minimum. That's exactly what they are: a demonstration of going above and beyond the minimum to improve yourself and the industry. In the same way as further education is an investment in yourself, so is professional registration. Just remember that there are annual fees associated with keeping the letters, otherwise you'll face a potential reassessment cost.

So, if you're an employer who's hiring and reviewing lots of CVs that pass across your desk, who's going to stand out more – Candidate A or Candidate B EngTech MIET?

CHAPTER 12

SAFETY

Mental Health

Imagine a scenario in which you're working on a large construction site. You, like everyone else at some point in their life, have issues going on at home. You want to chat to the people you've worked with, some of them for years, but you don't feel it's an environment where you can be open and talk in an emotional way. This carries on for days, weeks, months or even years. One day, you decide that you can't take it any more and decide to end your life.

This scenario is true for so many in the construction industry. The construction industry has a suicide rate that's three times higher than the national average.

Poor mental health in the construction industry has reached a point where it has recently begun to be dealt with. The machismo-laden, testosterone-filled industry of yesteryear is now fading away. There are stresses put on everyone within the construction industry. Long working hours – particularly in the winter months, when you're leaving home in darkness and returning home in darkness, thus spending little time with your loved ones and children – can have a great impact on your state of mind.

Electricians will face many stresses. Perhaps it's down to the basic installation work, such as not being able to install a cable because of a structural clash, or running over on the programme and having a boss breathing down your neck. It could be that you're the boss and you're seeing the costs go up, but the invoice isn't moving with them. Maybe you're a sole trader or the owner of a business that's been in operation for a long time and is facing going into liquidation. Every problem is just as valid as the one before it.

Stepping into a project management position, whether it's in a small or large business, does add another layer of complexity. With increased complexity comes stress. Multi-layering the need to manage people and push a job to completion, on budget and on time, is very rarely achieved, but it's always the aim. Typically, understanding this comes with experience.

Contractors are now employing mental health first aiders, which is one of the biggest steps within the industry in recent times towards addressing this issue. In the same way as a first aid practitioner will attend to your physical health, a mental health first aider is someone who can listen to you; they have the appropriate training to understand how to best help someone who's in distress, whatever the reason.

Many charities, such as Mind and the Samaritans, now focus on these areas of industry, providing an ear for those in need of someone to talk to. Much of the time, just talking to someone can relieve the stress and burden. The number of suicides is on the rise. It's easy to talk, so don't let whatever is stressing you out become too much. There's always a helping hand out there. Suicide isn't inevitable and is preventable.

One other aspect of working on a construction site that's associated with mental health is the banter...

Banter

"If you can't have a laugh, don't bother coming to work!" This was one of the first phrases uttered to me when beginning my own apprenticeship journey. The trades have long had a reputation for having a laugh.

Whether it's mocking each other, the work or simply playing pranks, there are many sites up and down the country where enjoying each other's company can be a pleasure. Working together as part of a team can build lifelong friendships. However, working together to achieve a project can be tough, but when it's done with a smile on your face, it makes work enjoyable.

It's always important to never let the banter go too far. There will be occasions where someone oversteps the mark. Everybody has their own personal line in the sand. The introductory hazing of apprentices can and does go on. There's a line between banter and bullying, so it's important to keep an eye out for this. If you're locking someone into a tool chest, then maybe you should step back and think about your actions.

Not suffering from poor mental health is becoming just as vital as having good physical health. If banter is making someone feel sad or uneasy, then it has potentially crossed the line into bullying.

Many will enjoy a weekly visit to the café to suitably clog up some arteries with a full English breakfast together. Others might unwind by having a beer in a sunny pub garden. Spending time together outside of the pressures of the job can certainly build bridges and make communication between people easier when inside it.

One thing is true, though: if you enter a construction site for work, you'll need a thick skin.

Risk Assessment Method Statements (RAMS)

From a commercial and industrial perspective, the culture of safety within the construction industry has changed in recent memory. The "where there's blame, there's a claim" culture fully engulfed society in the early 2000s. It wasn't that risk assessments and method statements didn't exist; rather, it might have been that the methodologies were unclear. Experience and knowledge were more heavily relied upon to complete a task that said person was trained to do. However, a method statement (which provides the step-by-step methodology of how to perform a task safely) would catch and detail the works' nuances that aren't critical to a fundamental understanding of the task at hand.

There's been an increase in awareness regarding qualifications for people working on the tools. There are five to ten qualifications that any one person needs to be a qualified electrician on a construction site in the 21st century.[19] In addition to all the electrical qualifications, you'll also need an ECS gold card, first aid training, SSSTS, powered access equipment training from IPAF, and mobile tower and podium training from PASMA. All of these build a person's safety profile.

Method statements have become more detailed in recent years. They're almost providing detailed instructions to a level at which someone with very little training could follow them. This isn't a bad thing! It does mean that the person completing the task has a point of reference – which they can read, review and even amend – along with a point-of-work risk assessment, task briefing or other mechanism to change safety documentation. It's important to remember that these documents are put in place for a person's safety. The methodology is there to be followed. Many might sign the safety documentation without fully reading it. Others might not sign it at all. Therein lies the blame, but you might not be able to claim.

Risk assessments are again self-explanatory; they assess the hazards and associated risk in each situation, which is the likelihood of that hazard coming to fruition and causing you harm. Let's work through a simple scenario. When you're walking in the rain, what's the likelihood of getting wet? It's certain. And because it's certain to happen, we need to do something about it. So, we take an umbrella; this is our personal protective equipment (PPE) in this instance, and we've mitigated the hazard of getting wet, reducing its likelihood and thereby removing the risk.

The domestic market is making slower progress in this regard, and it still relies on knowledge, understanding and competence in relation to safety. There are always spectrums of implementation, as with anything, and many small businesses are implementing high levels of safety on domestic construction sites. There will also be those who are implementing nothing. It doesn't take a genius to see which one is more likely to end up at the local hospital's accident and emergency department!

It's important to ensure your own safety and that of others. Always speak up if you're uncomfortable. We all want to go home at the end of the day!

Personal Protective Equipment (PPE)

There are a few misconceptions regarding PPE. In every situation, if you can remove a hazard and not even need to consider PPE, then take the appropriate action to do so.

Whenever you sign on to a RAMS, you're acknowledging what the document says. That could be the number and type of hazards presented to you, how you'll safely complete a task, where the nearest hospital is and who the nearest first aider is, amongst many other things. You'll also review the PPE required to complete the task. It's important to understand that many are educated "on the job" when it comes to PPE.

The PPE you'll wear will relate to the hazard that couldn't be removed. It's always important to remember that PPE is the last line of defence. So if you're working on a construction site and there's scaffolding work going on above you, for example, it's likely you'll be required to wear a hard hat. The responsibility will fall on you to behave correctly, wear your PPE appropriately and check your PPE is fit for purpose before engaging in your work. If it isn't, don't use it and ask for another. Cost isn't a consideration when it comes to safety.

Social pressure on construction sites is a real thing. It may sound somewhat childish, like being at school, but the bygone era of "toughness" and "cracking on" still very much exists. There has been a massive culture change on British construction sites in the last few decades. The influx of the "where there's blame, there's a claim" culture has resulted in many lawsuits for lifelong injuries, even minor one, where employers haven't fulfilled their role as a duty holder – and rightfully so.

We've seen the development in construction of an increased awareness of issues that pose a risk to health. Warning signs have been developed that detail what PPE you must wear when entering dedicated areas or sites. This is supported by the JIB CSCS and ECS tests, in which it is key for the individual to interpret what both PPE sign content and colour mean and what action to take as a result.

The PPE an electrician will wear might include insulated gloves, eye protection, respiratory masks, knee pads and steel toe cap boots. Buying steel toe cap boots with midsole protection is invaluable. The number of nails and screws stepped on will testify to this being a good purchase. Hard hats are also commonplace throughout the construction industry.

If your work is more industrial in nature, you might wear fireproof overalls. If you're working with LVAs, such as motor control centres (MCCs), then you might consider wearing arc flash switching PPE. This will include extensively tested PPE (such as face masks) that's compliant with a host of additional standards to keep you safe in the event of a release of energy (a big bang).

When your PPE becomes damaged or unusable, don't persist in using it. Request a replacement and get it changed and. Defective PPE won't protect anyone or prevent anything from potentially doing harm.

There are many more aspects to PPE. For example, if you work in hazardous areas, you may require a gas detector. It doesn't end at what you're wearing. It also doesn't end with you. If you see others not following the requirements, speak out. *Everybody* wants to go home at the end of the day.

Electrical Safety First

Electrical Safety First is a UK-based charity dedicated to promoting electrical safety awareness. Established in 2003, the organisation plays a role in educating the public, professionals and policymakers about the importance of electrical safety in homes, workplaces and other environments.

Historically, it might be slightly confusing, given that Electrical Safety First used to be the National Inspection Council for Electrical Installations & Contractors (NICEIC), but we won't go into all its history.

The primary mission of Electrical Safety First is to improve electrical safety standards and practices across the UK. It aims to achieve this by raising awareness of potential electrical hazards, providing expert advice and guidance, and advocating for better safety regulations and standards, thus reducing the number of accidents and preventing electrical-related fires and incidents.

Electrical Safety First conducts educational campaigns to inform the public about electrical hazards and safe practices. It develops resources, guides and videos to reach out, endeavouring to ensure that as many as possible understand the risks associated with electricity and how to stay safe.

The charity actively conducts research and collects data on electrical incidents and accidents. By analysing trends and identifying the common causes of electrical accidents, it can tailor its educational initiatives and lobby for targeted safety improvements.

Electrical Safety First also provides training and resources to electricians, engineers and other professionals in the electrical industry. By enhancing their knowledge and skills, it hopes to contribute to safer electrical installations and maintenance practices.

As a charity, it campaigns for improved consumer protection measures, emphasising the importance of purchasing electrical products from reputable sources and raising awareness about the dangers of counterfeit or substandard electrical items. It works closely with government bodies, regulators and industry stakeholders to influence policies and regulations related to electrical safety.

It provides a wealth of online resources, including safety guides, checklists and informative articles, which are available to everyone free of charge. It also offers a helpline for individuals seeking expert advice and support on electrical safety matters.

By raising awareness, advocating for safer regulations, and educating the public and professionals, the charity plays a crucial role within the electrical industry.

Not every electrician might use the resources of Electrical Safety First, but with a presence on social media, it provides easy access to its marketing campaigns and information on the topical issues it's promoting. Staying on top of industry developments is key to keeping ahead of the curve!

Asbestos

Asbestos is more than just a small town in Canada. It's one of the deadliest minerals on the planet. In the last century, the number of applications for asbestos grew rapidly. It doesn't dissolve in water or evaporate. It has fantastic characteristics –

such being resistant to heat, fire and chemical degradation – as well as being mechanically strong.

It seeped its way into many parts of society, and it's only in recent times that we in the UK have recognised its carcinogenic properties. You might find it in pipe insulation, flooring, tiling, and appliances such as ovens, coffee pots and hairdryers. Large parts of the world are yet to even recognise its effect on health.

The most common interface where a domestic electrician may encounter asbestos is in walls and ceilings, or possibly even in fuse cartridge holders for the old BS-88-style fuse boards. For a period of recent history, asbestos was introduced into plaster for its quick-setting properties and the ability to make shapes and patterns on the ceilings of every day homes. This is commonly known as Artex. Artex, amongst all the types of asbestos and products, has a lower risk rating. However, over many years of drilling downlights, working in lofts and chasing walls, the number of exposures can add up – leading to health issues.

The two main effects asbestos has on health are the lung-related diseases known as mesothelioma and asbestosis. Unfortunately, it isn't possible to cure either mesothelioma or asbestosis. Either of these can be a painful way to exit this mortal coil. As with many asbestos-related health issues, the symptoms won't appear for many years, maybe even decades. Prevention is the *only* cure.

There are many types of asbestos. The predominant ones are these:

- Chrysotile (white)
- Amosite (brown)
- Crocidolite (blue)

All types of asbestos are dangerous if inhaled or ingested.

Asbestos awareness training is something that every electrician should undertake. Asbestos has reached far and wide into global products. Whilst production and implementation may have stopped in the UK, it still has an incredible presence.

When entering commercial and industrial buildings to undertake work, you can request to see (if there is one – and there should be) the asbestos register. In there, it should detail the types and locations of any asbestos present.

Masks are important when working as an electrician, as it isn't just asbestos that's a health risk. Dust, wood fibres and loft insulation, amongst other things, can all cause health issues.

The more time passes, the more we can ascertain from the data and correlate it to long-term health issues being experienced by those in certain trades.

Overall, the key for electricians is to approach any work involving older buildings or potential asbestos-containing materials with caution and to always prioritise safety. If there's any doubt about the presence of asbestos or how to handle it safely, don't touch it. Seek professional advice, and assistance is vital. There are many professional companies who can now test for asbestos, provide results within 24 hours and remove it safely.

CHAPTER 13

CHALLENGES

Quality

There are some things that just can't be taught. Producing quality work is something that goes beyond compliance. Learning the rules and regulations is one thing, but understanding the nuances of what makes a job look good is another entirely.

From a domestic customer's point of view, quality will be something entirely different. Turning up on time, completing the works promptly, tidying up after yourself and issuing the certification promptly after completion are all good qualities. Whilst cost will also factor into a customer's version of what quality is, with a tradesperson – as with any other product in the world – you get what you pay for. The mantra of "buy cheap, buy twice" is never truer than when a bad installation has been completed.

Then there's the tougher nut to crack: quality amongst peers. A small aspect of this will be in the eye of the beholder. However, over the generations ,specific skills have been handed down that electricians either will or won't have. A good example of this would be installing steel galvanised conduit. In the electrical industry, there will be those who've put in steel conduit day in, day out for years. They'll thread, bubble set, bend and contort it into all directions. It will flow and be flawless, not require any running couplers (unless desired), and be perfectly re-galvanised where scuffed or marked. These skills are somewhat taught in college, but they're 100% honed on the construction sites of the country.

There's an art to dressing cabling into containment systems, particularly ones where the cabling is to be visible, such as cable tray or ladder. Neatly following their bending radius in their groups can look fantastic. But if not done well, it's immediately noticeable. Luckily for electricians, most installations will take place in walls, ceilings and voids, and they never see the light of day – or a customer's eyes. But future electricians will access it for future maintenance, and if it isn't done well, they'll curse the sky red if their life is made difficult and problems are found.

The industry has struggled with quality in recent years, due to some of the issues already mentioned in this book. Short-course-trained personnel completing work that's below the standards required for regulations, let alone the harsh judgements of their peers, have left customers frustrated and many in the industry pointing fingers at those companies and individuals who can have a positive influence, demanding they do more.

Larger businesses in various sectors will take quality more seriously. They'll implement controls and procedures. This can lead to quality management systems and the external verification of those systems under ISO 9001, the standard for quality. These systems can be applied to companies of any size, although the external assessment and annual maintenance of these approvals isn't necessarily something smaller-income businesses will want to do.

Audits are a vital aspect of quality. Checking and inspecting not only your work but also every aspect of how your business operates to ensure standards are maintained can be key to keeping standards high.

Quality documentation is also something to consider. When simply looking at an electrical installation certificate, any electrician worth their salt will be able to spot mistakes immediately. This can range from tick boxes being completed incorrectly for an installation to circuit information not being inserted correctly. Always try to write and review your documentation as if you were the person reading it in a year's time.

Whether you're self-employed or employed, having a quality approach to everything you do will create a good reputation, both internally to the business and externally with customers.

Advertising

Advertising is an ever-changing game in the modern world. Businesses are always finding new strategies, markets and locations in which to advertise their services.

For the average electrician, advertising via local community newsletters or magazines has almost become a thing of the past, although there will be many who still use this method that are doing very well in generating revenue and interest.

Social media is now a significant way many use to obtain their day-to-day business. Whether that's advertising on local community Facebook pages or creating their own Facebook pages, X (formerly Twitter) profiles or Instagram posts detailing some of their previous work (and that's where quality comes into play).

Registering a business with Google is an excellent way of businesses making themselves known to the public that doesn't have any direct advertising costs associated with it. Not only will this then provide hits within people's local search engine results but it can also link them to websites, contact details and reviews.

Gaining reviews is a perfect way of demonstrating your reliability, quality and customer service. This is effectively your previous customers selling your services to new potential customers, at no cost.

Many lead-generation apps have expanded into the construction industry in recent years. These can be an expensive way of obtaining work with no guarantee from a client that an order will be placed. There will be those who understand how to work these systems to their advantage and have made a success of it, but beware.

Word of mouth is still largely the primary way lots of electricians generate sales leads for their businesses. Everyone knows someone who wants the services of an electrician or tradesperson. Good service feedback from one customer directly to another will almost always result in an enquiry.

Another method of advertising is to utilise your own vehicle as a billboard. Most companies will now do this automatically. Branding can be critical to this. Recognisable logos are always beneficial, as are easy-to-remember company names. Including the logos associated with any memberships and/or affiliations for the business, such as a competent person scheme, will immediately inspire confidence. There are many sign-writing companies out there, and this is one of the most cost-effective ways of promoting your business whilst on the move.

Self-presentation is also an important aspect of advertising your business. Arriving at a client's property or business in clean, branded workwear will go a long way to creating a professional image. Many working in the domestic sector might overlook this, but it can provide an advantage over other small businesses.

Ultimately, these are but a few of the potential ways for you to market your services. In an ever-competitive world, any advantage you can make the most of might just help keep your business afloat.

Community Engagement

One of the keys to success is engaging and interacting with others in your field. This can be someone of any skill level, at any point in their journey. Everyone has something to offer.

The traditional days of socialising with your colleagues and friends down the pub are still very much alive within the construction industry. The half-day Friday to socialise and have a beer or two is a great way to build a team and foster better relationships (as long as you're drinking responsibly). There's also the weekly ritual of going for a full English fry-up.

Many people working in the construction industry – particularly domestically – will work solitarily. They may or may not have an apprentice. This can be a very lonely place, especially when you're put under stress, so it's important to engage with others in your industry community.

Most will do this in some form by turning to the world of social media. Social media within the electrical industry has grown massively, as it has generally throughout society. Over half the population of the planet now use social media in some form. Within the electrical sector, there has been a rise in YouTube channels, with people of all skills and levels sharing technical content – some of a quality most tutors in a college would be happy with (with some of them actually being tutors, by the way!) – alongside sharing their daily lives and what it means to be an electrician completing a certain aspect of work.

Additionally, there has been an influx of podcasts in recent years with many – even including big-name brands and manufacturers – entering the space. The content ranges across a wide spectrum of topics whilst still being industry specific, and it incorporates news, education, conversation and entertainment. These are all opportunities for you to absorb information on some level and to develop continuously your understanding of the industry, but why not be entertained along the way?

Alongside listening to podcasts, every domestic building site in the country will typically have a radio somewhere in the vicinity. Big-name tool brands have ventured into the world of radios to provide durable radios that ensure the trades are never without their tunes. In recent years, we've seen more and more DAB radio stations appearing, including construction-industry-specific channels that facilitate call-in guests sharing stories and learning together. However, radios and music of all forms have now typically disappeared from the commercial and industrial construction sites. This is mainly due to the implications on health and safety, which is understandable. Logically, this should follow into the domestic sector.

There are platforms available on which specific chat rooms and conversational threads (or forums) can also be utilised. The IET has its own platforms if you want to be very industry specific and know reliably that you're going to get the right answer.

You might have similar experiences on social media platforms such as X (formerly Twitter), Facebook and others. There will be many people to follow, connect with and learn from.

There's simply an abundance now that wasn't available previously, even in recent memory, thanks to the internet. There's never been a better time to train to be an electrician with so much content available on anything and everything associated with the electrical industry.

If you're contemplating joining the industry (and I'm assuming you are or already have as you're reading this book) and haven't yet left the job you're in, as you're scared to make the leap, or if your careers advisor at school just isn't helping, a quick online search will put the whole electrical industry at your fingertips.

CHAPTER 14

THE FUTURE

The Environment and Sustainability

The words "environment" and "sustainability" can mean many things within the electrical industry. More recently, the increased introduction of renewables into the domestic installation market has piqued interest in these previously quiet sectors of the electrical industry.

Sustainability means more than the installations an electrician completes – it also encompasses their business operations. Businesses are being challenged harder than ever before to make their operations green. This can be anything from the products they purchase and install to the packaging they come within. The changeover from halogen lamps to LEDs has already occurred in the previous decades, and LED lighting has brought down energy usage, making it a fraction of the cost.

Ever-increasing amounts of products are now coming in cardboard or recyclable packaging. Businesses monitor their carbon footprint and avoid making less environmentally friendly choices wherever possible, including steering clear of single-use plastics.

The irony is that electricians have been recycling cable for time immemorial. With copper stripped from cable fetching a premium price at most metal recycling centres, scrap cable has always been a way of an electrician earning slightly more on their working day. If you can be bothered to strip a cable down to its copper (particularly if it has a large cross-sectional area), then recycling a substantial amount will achieve a nice bonus for you.

The disposal of fluorescent lighting tubes has historically been an issue. These are products that contain toxic gases – including argon, mercury and phosphorus. For the occasional job, most electrical wholesalers do take these in for recycling under the Waste Electrical and Electronic Equipment Directive (WEEE) regulations. If you're regularly removing this type of lamp, your business may need to consider having its own dedicated fluorescent tube recycling bin.

The whole-life cost of a product and its installation is a factor not everyone considers or sells to potential clients. Some domestic customers will even go out of their way to purchase the products themselves, believing they'll get it cheaper than wholesale. Ultimately, they choose a lower quality product for a lower price. This shouldn't be a problem for an electrician. If the client wishes to waive any guarantees that you were willing to offer with your own product, that's their right to decide.

When that product fails in two years' time, rather than the 10-year lifespan of your alternative product, it's simple maths. An electrician revisiting five times versus the single up-front installation cost will show the whole-life cost being lower when the product's installed. I'm grossly oversimplifying here, but the premise really is that clear-cut. In some cases, the client will blame the electrician and not the product they selected, and therefore they'll move on to seek services elsewhere in future. When deciding on your business strategy, it's worth considering how to deal with this type of customer.

Electric Vehicles (EVs)

When discussing the environment and sustainability, we can't avoid discussing fossil fuels. Fossil fuels have become a big target of the environmental agenda, and the rise of EVs has been a fast one.

The future of our planet has long been discussed in many a news article. Activism is high. The electrical industry is endeavouring to move with the times. The rapid technological developments are taking the regulations for a ride, and no one really knows where it's going next.

Governments are setting national targets, with terms such as "net zero" being thrown around. Whether these targets will be hit, manipulated or are even realistic isn't for me to discuss within this book. They are, however, influencing industry, the economy and electrical installations up and down the country.

EVs are now on the public agenda, whether it's government grants for homeowners, councils spending on charge points or supermarket chains providing charge points. Where there's massive sudden spending, it can create a commercial gap that needs to be filled: a gold rush.

With electrical energy being a crucial aspect of the future, becoming self-sufficient and avoiding the huge costs associated with energy suppliers will be a necessity.

Homes are very quickly having solar panels, battery storage, ground-source heat pumps and much more installed. Renewable energy is being included in the plans for the national infrastructure, with large swathes of fields in the country now being utilised for solar and wind power generation. This does feel somewhat at odds with the very nature of renewable energy.

The safety associated with EVs has been a hot topic within the industry, highlighting many other issues within the required infrastructure, such as the loss of neutral current, alongside neutral current being diverted into homes from the UK's power networks. Including technology such as O-PEN devices has become a staple of more and more EV installations.

Technology is being developed from all angles – not just for the EVs themselves but for the chargers too, which can now have the ability to monitor not only the car's charge level but also household operational load levels. Using current transformers, they can reduce EV charging time whilst high-load items are utilised within the property, particularly where there's a risk of reaching the maximum demand, etc. These high-load items are things such as showers, ovens, induction hobs and more in the modern domestic home.

There are also cheaper, less sophisticated products that achieve the same output but don't necessarily make information available on your mobile phone via wireless network signals.

If you've been asked to install an EV charging point, the best place to start is always with a survey of the property or site. UK Power Networks (UKPN) has a right of refusal for EV charging installations. For any installation that will increase demand to be over the 60A maximum demand threshold, an application is required in advance of completing any installation work. Even where the 60A maximum demand isn't exceeded, approval is still required and must be completed within a notification period of 28 days post-installation. The application form will require information about the installation, such as details of the incoming fuse, voltage measurements and more. It's very worthwhile to ensure you conduct a thorough inspection in advance of quoting for and completing such installations, including verifying the condition of the consumer unit, protective devices and main bonding conductors – all day-to-day activities that electricians undertake anyway.

One of the major considerations in such an installation is the earthing system of the UKPN supply into the property. It's worth noting that within the UKPN's earthing specification (EDS006 B.4) it states that all TN-S supplies are to be considered TNC-S, due to concentric cables being used within UKPN's network.[20] This means that just assessing the visible supply head in the property is a flawed approach. For the layperson, this is the combined neutral and earth supply.

The next consideration is the type of vehicle and mode of charging that's required. Typically, we expect to see a battery or hybrid vehicle, but it's always worth checking the manufacturer's guidance and instructions to see if any specifics are required. Dedicated circuits are a must, as the mode-one type of charging (having a non-dedicated circuit and socket outlet) is all but outlawed. Most chargers will operate in the 7.4kW load range with a mode-three type of charging installation, giving roughly a three to six-hour charge time.

Managing the maximum power demand is something that's not only of interest to the homeowner but also to the National Grid. With ever-increasing demand, having a flexible network where you can divert power at will to where it's required will be vital. Waking up to find your car hasn't charged might be a reality of the future.

All of this can be information overload for an apprentice, so it's always important to remember Rome wasn't built in a day.

You may think of your EV like a giant battery that can constantly be emptied and recharged. However, if you're a prosumer, what if the battery becomes a source of supply for the house? Running a bit short on energy this evening? Could you use the battery you've left in your EV to supplement your household loads? Well, yes, you can.

The Prosumer

As a relatively new term within the electrical industry, "prosumer" is defined within BS 7671 as "a party which can be both a producer and a consumer of electrical energy."[21] It's a given that, unless you live completely remotely in the middle of a forest, you're going to consume electrical energy. This industry development gives homeowners the ability to produce and store their own electrical energy.

Whilst solar panels have long been available and utilised by homeowners, never has the uptake for green energy been so high in the domestic market as it is now in the 21st century. As has more than been demonstrated in recent years, the destabilising of the energy markets is a concern for whole the country, let alone individually.

Unfortunately, living in the UK brings the associated climate with it. With frequent clouds, rain and poor visibility, you're going to need to consume energy from local networks. However, the prosumer has other technology at their disposal to further reduce this consumption: battery storage installed in domestic settings. This facilitates storing energy gathered from the sun to be utilised later. It also enables cheaper rates of electricity to be maximised. Economy 7 heating systems have long used cheaper overnight energy rates, when there's less demand on energy networks.

Introducing batteries into the domestic space does present a question, and it's one that will be answered in the many years to come: should the use of direct current (DC) installations within domestic settings be revisited? Most appliances now operate utilising extra-low-voltage DC supplies. If we're going to be generating DC electricity via solar panels and storing it in DC batteries, only to invert it to the alternating current (AC) (creating significant efficiency losses) used in the home, before converting it back to DC to charge your mobile phone or even an EV, then it isn't the most efficient method. Will the future accommodate AC and DC circuits within installations? Only time will tell.

Selling back your energy to the network is relatively new for consumers. The price points are significantly lower when it's bought back. Most homeowners are opting to utilise their own energy rather than send it back into the National Grid. How this will be managed in the future, with networks potentially being required to call on homeowners to "borrow" their energy, isn't yet understood fully, but it's potentially something to develop in the future.

Installations can opt out of this bi-directional exchange of energy by operating in what's known as "island mode". This describes when an installation isn't connected to the energy networks and provides – through whatever means of generation – sufficient energy to support its own installation. These types require an understanding of private supply requirements, TT earthing arrangements, RCDs and more.

When considering these requirements in parallel with EVs, battery storage, solar systems, heat pumps and smart homes, the domestic installer is going to be stretched way beyond anything they've completed in the last few decades – far beyond the ring final and lighting circuits.

Smart Homes

We've all seen the movies about the future, and in many, there will be glimpses of the smart homes that may come to exist if installations are pushed to an extreme. *Star Wars, Blade Runner* and *Minority Report* all feature homes with automatic operation through touch screens and voice activation. This is now a reality for many homes and buildings up and down the country.

There are some who still don't trust the clap-on light. They'll ultimately be left behind.

Appliances, lighting and systems in the home with automatic controls are increasingly being selected by customers. The use of wireless technology has jumped tenfold with the betterment of Wi-Fi in the home. However, the more complex systems are still using good old-fashioned copper wire.

Most homes up and down the country might have simply put their toe in the water with this technology, opting for solutions ranging from video doorbells to fire alarm detectors, each connecting via your mobile phone.

There are some homes that take this another step further by introducing the "fancy" lighting systems with stylish LED lighting, in tuneable colours, which are hidden in various ways throughout the property to provide a seamless lighting system. Added to this are detection systems to understand if/when a person is present in a room. Installations can range from the simple passive infrared (PIR) sensors for detecting motion to the outright ludicrous temperature detection sensors.

Products have long been progressing with regard to integral technology. Almost every external garden lighting fixture will now include a variety of controls. The obvious one being photocell detection for when the sun goes down. Most street lighting installations will operate in this way. They may then include PIR detection. However, you don't want your garden lit all night. Add to that a timer for how long you want the light to remain operational for once motion has been detected. Finally, upscale this to incorporate every light inside your home, and it can soon become a comprehensive system.

Beyond controlling your simple home entertainment system and your television, home cinemas can now be installed even in the smallest of lounges. They include unfolding screens and paper-thin televisions, which are wall mounted to not impact the space. Audio systems providing surround sound, which were previously confined to the homes of movie buffs, are now being utilised up and down the country.

Controlling appliances remotely is another aspect gathering steam within the industry. It's a big development in the efforts to save energy. You can do anything from remotely operating your washing machine (though I'm not sure what the benefit of doing this is) to closing your curtains. The wealthier members of society who are able to use these controls when considering swimming pools, saunas and other extraneous systems requiring lots of energy will benefit greatly from this approach.

These are usually data-heavy systems with full control panels and, potentially, even servers. Specific manufacturers are leading the market with their programmable controllers. Hardwiring ethernet throughout the house is usually the best way to guarantee there are no Wi-Fi issues.

> The average household is beginning to benefit from smart-home technology, with more investments being made alongside clean, local energy generation. Energy saving is only good if you're not wasting any.

The biggest contributor to energy usage in a UK home is heating! Staying warm has been a human concern since the dawn of time. In the UK, we've made use of many heating methods for our homes throughout modern history. We have immersion heaters, boilers, storage heaters and underfloor heating – all of which are basic circuits with thermostat control.

In recent years, we've seen a big push – and a government-incentivised push – for the use of air- and ground-source heat pumps. Whilst these are part of a trend, managing the ground works is an installation cost many don't necessarily want to invest in alongside maintenance. Air-source heat pumps have negated this issue by being mounted above ground.

To get back to your electrical training, heating plans are a vital part of the learning curve of installations for anyone in the electrical industry. As an apprentice, you're likely to be introduced to this domestically very early. It's very seldom implemented in the criteria of an apprenticeship at colleges, so on-the-job learning will be vital. Depending on which branch you sit your exam in, an S- or Y-plan heating system is included in the assessment criteria in the aforementioned AM2.

Entering this exam without having gained prior experience can make it extra challenging. It's always a good idea to utilise the preparation day offered before the AM2 exams if you're unfamiliar with any aspects of the test.

CONCLUSION

Electricity Kills – Take it Seriously

As electricians, we're the unsung heroes who ensure our modern world stays illuminated and connected. However, amidst the marvels of electricity lies an inherent danger that can threaten your safety and well-being.

Stating the obvious, electricians will have dangerous encounters with electricity, but this doesn't necessarily have to result in an electric shock. A common phrase you'd have heard in the electrical industry even as recently as 20 years ago is along the lines of "Every electrician will get an electric shock at some point." It was perceived as a rite of passage. There was a false sense of security amongst the trade, that everyone receives shocks, but everyone lives to tell the tale. This simply isn't true.

There have been media campaigns to drive up the implementation and use of safe isolation procedures and equipment, particularly in the domestic sector, where there's less governance.

Protective devices and electrical system designs have included safe limits of exposure for the human body for some time. In the event of a fault, 50V is considered the maximum safe voltage to touch (ignoring the recent increase to 70V associated with EV installations) because it isn't sufficient electrical energy to disrupt bodily functions. It's important to remember that we, as human beings, are walking batteries with electrical signals being discharged all throughout our body.

The industry expects its RCDs to disconnect within anticipated times (pretty much instantaneously) in the event of a fault, even at these extra-low voltages.

There are many factors that can determine the outcome of an electric shock, with the current being one of the forerunners. Typically, throughout the domestic sector in the UK, RCDs will have a 30mA rating. It's well understood that even up to 20mA of current can be painful and cause loss of muscle control. Now imagine being on a tall stepladder whilst terminating a lighting fixture in a home when such a shock occurs. Sometimes, it isn't the electric shock that kills, but the fall afterwards.

Every day, electricians walk into new environments, new installations, new parameters, and new risks and hazards.

Take it seriously. Electricity can kill.

ABBREVIATIONS

2D	Two-dimensional
3D	Three-dimensional
AC	Alternating current
ACB	Air circuit breaker
AM2	Achievement Measurement 2
BMS	Building management system
BIM	Building information modelling
BS	British Standard
CEng	Chartered engineer
CIBSE	Chartered Institute of Building Service Engineers
CPD	Continuous professional development
CSCS	Construction Skills Certification Scheme
CV	Curriculum vitae
DC	Direct current
ECA	Electrical Contractors' Association
EngTech	Engineering technician
EV	Electric vehicle

FIET	Fellow of the Institution of Engineering and Technology
HNC	Higher National Certificate
HND	Higher National Diploma
HSE	Health and Safety Executive
HVAC	Heating, ventilation and air conditioning
IEC	International Electrotechnical Commission
IEng	Incorporated engineer
IET	Institution of Engineering and Technology
IPAF	International Powered Access Federation
JIB	Joint Industry Board
JIB ECS	Joint Industry Board Electrotechnical Certification Scheme
JPEL	Joint Power and Electrical
LVA	Low-voltage assembly
MCB	Miniature circuit breaker
MCC	Motor control centre
MCCB	Moulded case circuit breaker
MEWP	Mobile elevated working platform
MIET	Member of the Institution of Engineering and Technology
NAPIT	National Association of Professional Inspectors and Testers
NAPIT EICR	National Association of Professional Inspectors and Testers Electrical Installation Condition Reports
NEC	New Engineering Contract
NICEIC	National Inspection Council for Electrical Installation Contracting
NVQ	National vocational qualification
PASMA	Prefabricated Access Suppliers' and Manufacturers' Association
PIR	Passive infrared

PAT	Portable appliance testing
PPE	Personal protective equipment
RAMS	Risk Assessment Method Statement
RCBO	Residual current breakers with overload protection
RCD	Residual current device
SME	Small to medium-sized enterprise
SMSTS	Site Manager Safety Training Scheme
SSSTS	Site Supervisor Safety Training Scheme
STEM	Science, technology, engineering and mathematics
TMIET	Technician member of the Institution of Engineering and Technology
UKPN	UK Power Networks
UPS	Uninterruptable power supply
UV	Ultraviolet
VAT	Value added tax
WEEE	Waste Electrical and Electronic Equipment Directive

REFERENCES

1. Gladwell, M. (2009). *Outliers*. London, UK: Penguin.

2. Horne, B. (2022, May 27). *How many businesses fail in the first year in the UK?* NerdWallet. Retrieved from https://www.nerdwallet.com/uk/business/start-up-failure-statistics/

3. Horne, B. (2022, May 27). *How many businesses fail in the first year in the UK?* NerdWallet. Retrieved from https://www.nerdwallet.com/uk/business/start-up-failure-statistics/

4. Camden, B. (2022, March 21). 2020/21 apprenticeship achievement rate hits 57.7% – and just 51.8% for standards. *Feweek*. Retrieved from https://feweek.co.uk/2020-21-apprenticeship-achievement-rate-hit-57-7-and-just-51-8-for-standards/

5. *The Electricity at Work Regulations 1989* (2015, April 6). Retrieved from https://www.hse.gov.uk/pubns/priced/hsr25.pdf

6. *The Electricity at Work Regulations 1989* (2015, April 6). Retrieved from https://www.hse.gov.uk/pubns/priced/hsr25.pdf

7. Gov.uk (2022, December 22). *Academic year 2021/22: Apprenticeships and traineeships*. Retrieved from https://explore-education-statistics.service.gov.uk/find-statistics/apprenticeships-and-traineeships/2021-22

8. Gov.uk (2022, December 22). *Academic year 2021/22: Apprenticeships and traineeships*. Retrieved from https://explore-education-statistics.service.gov.uk/find-statistics/apprenticeships-and-traineeships/2021-22

9. Gov.uk (2022, December 22). *Academic year 2021/22: Apprenticeships and traineeships*. Retrieved from https://explore-education-statistics.service.gov.uk/find-statistics/apprenticeships-and-traineeships/2021-22

10. Beal, A.N. (2007, January). CDM Regulations: 12 years of pain but little gain. *ICE Proceedings Civil Engineering, 160*(2), 82–88. Retrieved from https://www.researchgate.net/publication/245407835_CDM_Regulations_12_years_of_pain_but_little_gain#pf5

11. National Association of Professional Inspectors and Testers (2018). *NAPIT EICR Codebreakers*. Mansfield, UK: National Association of Professional Inspectors and Testers.

12. The Institute of Engineering and Technology (2022). *Guidance note 3: Inspection & testing*. Stevenage, UK: The Institute of Engineering and Technology.

13. The Institute of Engineering and Technology (2022). *On-site guide* (8th ed.). Stevenage, UK: The Institute of Engineering and Technology.

14. The Institute of Engineering and Technology (2022). *On-site guide* (8th ed.). Stevenage, UK: The Institute of Engineering and Technology.

15. *The Electricity at Work Regulations 1989* (2015, April 6). Retrieved from https://www.hse.gov.uk/pubns/priced/hsr25.pdf

16. Companies House (2023, November 20). *Being a company director*. Gov.uk. Retrieved from https://www.gov.uk/guidance/being-a-company-director

17. Horne, B. (2022, May 27). *How many businesses fail in the first year in the UK?* NerdWallet. Retrieved from https://www.nerdwallet.com/uk/business/start-up-failure-statistics/

18. Peace, M. (2023, May). Corrigendum 2023 to BS 7671:2018+A2:2022. *Wiring Matters*, 95. Retrieved from https://electrical.theiet.org/wiring-matters/years/2023/95-may-2023/corrigendum-2023-to-bs-76712018plusa22022/

19. Joint Industry Board (2023). Section 4 Grading definitions. In *JIB Handbook*. Retrieved from https://www.jib.org.uk/documents/handbooks/19-48756-u-jib-handbook-interactive-ev15-79-92.pdf

20. Tucker, S. (2015). *Engineering design standard EDS 06-0017 Customer LV installation earthing design*. Scribd. Retrieved from https://www.scribd.com/document/339670643/EDS-06-0017-Customer-Installation-Earthing-Design-pdf

21. The Institute of Engineering and Technology (2022). *BS 7671 Requirements for electrical installations* (18th ed.). Stevenage, UK: The Institute of Engineering and Technology.

ABOUT THE AUTHOR

After starting as an electrical apprentice in 2006, Gary worked for a small to medium-sized electrical contractor that specialised in control systems and manufacturing bespoke control panels. He worked on a variety of projects, ranging from water treatment works and food production lines to hazardous-area installations for the national grid. He gained experience within the domestic sector by working all the evenings and weekends he could with other electricians outside his daily business.

After qualifying as an electrician, he undertook the City & Guilds 2391 inspection and testing qualification. At this time, he began to run several projects as a site supervisor for various clients, including the Environment Agency, for which Gary worked throughout the country.

During this period, he also undertook as many qualifications as he could to continue his professional development. This was in the form of health and safety qualifications with the National Examination Board in Occupational Safety and Health (NEBOSH) and a Higher National Diploma (HND) in the electronics and electrical field. Gary also became a member of the Institution of Engineering and Technology (IET) to assist in guiding his development.

After successfully delivering several projects, he took the opportunity to step into project management. Over the next few years, he delivered large-scale infrastructure projects such as sewage treatment works upgrades and maintenance contracts. In 2016, this culminated in him being made the managing director of the same business he'd started at as an apprentice.

In 2017, Gary founded his own electrical contracting business and worked primarily within the commercial and domestic sectors, completing rewires, inspection and testing, and various other works.

He was then offered the opportunity to join the Tideway project for the Bam, Morgan Singal and Balfour Beatty (BMB) joint venture for seven sites throughout London. Within 18 months, he'd been promoted to the Mechanical, Electrical, Instrumentation, Control and Automation (MEICA) design and installation manager, overseeing the design through many stages into construction, with various stakeholders involved.

In 2020, Gary became a chartered manager and fellow of the IET, validating the skills and engineering knowledge he'd gained in his career to date. This was shortly followed in 2021 by being awarded chartered manager status and becoming a fellow of the Chartered Managers Institute (CMI).

At that time, he also began to host industry podcast *Hit the Lights*, in which he spoke to guests throughout the electrical industry about their career journeys.

Gary is enthusiastic about the electrical industry and keen to share experiences and to raise awareness that some of the stigmas associated with becoming an electrician aren't necessarily what you might think – hence him writing this book.

He hopes you've enjoyed reading it as much as he enjoyed writing it and that you'll consider what the electrical industry can offer you.

You can contact Gary by email at Gary@theelecbook.co.uk or follow him on Instagram @garyalderceng.